Africa in Transformation

"Carlos Lopes is one of those rare characters who can combine intellectual excellence with strategic vision and still engage in policy making. In this book, readers will find an overview of Africa's profound transformation, interpreting changes ranging from traditional industries, to agro-businesses, to new advances in information and communication technology-based services and tourism. Lopes argues that Africa needs a clear inclusive growth strategy, supported by better institutions, regional synergies, and infrastructure to enable a leap forward. The complex politics involved in coordinating 54 countries within a continent indicates there will be no real prosperity without full commitment to diversity. Despite its tremendous economic potential, it remains critical to ensure that Africa's fast economic growth leaves less, not more, poor people behind, reversing past decades of underperformance. This essential book teaches that a prosperous Africa is not only good for Africans, but for the entire world."
—Glauco Arbix, *University of São Paulo, Brazil*

"Carlos Lopes is an economist with vast experience on Capacity Development, Political Affairs and Strategic Planning, with a background in academic and public sector institutions. He provides a good overview of the complexity of observed transitions in the continent, providing insights on the acceleration of industrialization as a key aspect of Africa's development transformation. In an easy and well managed use of playful metaphors, the 'sea' theme Lopes uses provides the reader with authentic navigation tools to identify what can be done to transform Africa. This book is in the must-read category for any student, scholar, practitioner and policymaker working on Africa."
—Alexandra A. Arkhangelskaya, *Russian Academy of Sciences, Russia*

"Africa is undergoing unprecedented changes and Carlos Lopes is the best person in the world to make sense of them all. His years of professional experience on the Continent combined with his deep intellectual knowledge have led leaders from across the world to seek his counsel. With *Africa in Transformation* Lopes makes his vast knowledge and keen insights available to everyone. This book is both a generous gift and a necessary tool for anyone seeking to understand Africa."
—Reuben Brigetty II, *George Washington University, USA* and *Council on Foreign Relations, USA*

"*Africa in Transformation* engages several African mega narratives and stitches together rich reflections on Africa's resilience and brazen self-renewal. Carlos Lopes interrogates the anatomy of the African experience in a methodical analysis uniting economic history and literary interludes to come to grips with the making of the current debates on the 'Africa rising' narrative. He does this in ten thought-through chapters linking the past and present, where structural economic transformation, climate change and the comparative political economy of late industrialization, particularly in China, take a centre stage. Below the surface is a people-centred book that energises the ethos of a binding social contract within and across states for the common good. Brilliantly counterintuitive, a must-read for everyone who cares about Africa's past, present and future."

—Mohamed Salih, *Erasmus University, the Netherlands*

"Africa has been so plagued and misrepresented by externally generated global descriptions and evaluations that it is hard to imagine an African scholar, even with the brilliant credentials of Carlos Lopes, capable of offering us today a synthesis, at one time rigorous and just, of the immense diversity of the continent. In this case, reality has proven stronger than imagination. Such a daunting task has been accomplished by the author so successfully and with so much wisdom and subtlety that this book is must read for any scholar, diplomat or policy maker concerned with Africa."

—Boaventura Sousa Santos, *University of Coimbra, Portugal* and *University of Wisconsin-Madison, USA*

"This is a magnificent book by Professor Carlos Lopes. Eloquently and succinctly Lopes describes the pathways for Africa's future economic transformation, pushing aside the old 'Africa Rising' or 'basket case' narrative, and providing nuance and insight in what is occurring in a continent of 54 countries. As Africa progresses with its Continental Free Trade Area this is a must read for international policy makers, academics and business people. Carlos Lopes describes how Africa's economic future will impact us all and why we all have a stake in ensuring success."

—Alex Vines OBE, *Chatham House, UK* and *Coventry University, UK*

Carlos Lopes

Africa in Transformation

Economic Development in the Age of Doubt

Carlos Lopes
Mandela School of Public Governance
University of Cape Town
Rondebosch, South Africa

ISBN 978-3-030-01290-8   ISBN 978-3-030-01291-5   (eBook)
https://doi.org/10.1007/978-3-030-01291-5

Library of Congress Control Number: 2018960929

Cover illustration: Natouche / iStock / Getty Images Plus

This Palgrave Macmillan imprint is published by the registered company Springer Nature Switzerland AG
The registered company address is: Gewerbestrasse 11, 6330 Cham, Switzerland

ACKNOWLEDGEMENTS

I would like to thank several people, including Hany Besada, Stefan Csordas, Charles Akong, Mayer Ngomesia, Adama Coulibaly, Chichi Bodart, Flavia Ba, Stephen Karingi, and Ottavia Pesce for their research assistance, along with Kojo Busia and Inderpal Dhiman for their support in procuring the materials that went into writing this book. Sandra Baffoe-Bonnie and Mestawet Mistir provided continuous support. I would also like to thank George Kararach for his editorial counselling and encouragement and Achim Steiner for the institutional support. The book could not have been finished without the generous conditions offered to me by the Oxford Martin School, Oxford University. When the book was already in production the news of the untimely death of Kofi Annan, one of the reviewers of this monograph, hit me hard. He was a constant source of inspiration. Finally, I would like to acknowledge the strength and energy offered to me by my wife, Maracimoni.

ABOUT THIS BOOK

This book is based on my reflections over the last few years on African developmental issues that were recently expressed in several blogs, speeches, and invited lectures across Africa. I want to thank all those who gave me the opportunity to share some of these materials before this volume was edited.

I have been trying to achieve three broad objectives: (a) to roll back an emerging trend in the debates on African development, which seems to downplay the challenges of the continent over the last two decades due to a rather simplistic, sometimes euphoric, narrative; (b) to expand the knowledge about the continent using historical and contextual insights hitherto not readily available to the general reader; and (c) to make practical suggestions to the policymaker on how to 'prioritise' changes in a complex, yet dynamic, continent.

This work is the culmination of four years of efforts leading the foremost development think tank and policy arm of the United Nations in the continent, the Economic Commission for Africa, based in Addis Ababa. It is an attempt to widen policy space and provide alternative thoughts on the full extent of opportunities and challenges in enabling the socio-economic transformation of Africa. It offers my insights on the acceleration of industrialisation as a key aspect of this transformation. For me, the very idea that industrialisation has been 'dropped' from the official development agenda for quite some time is unfortunate, given the attendant emphasis on trade as a goal, instead of an enabler. History suggests that the road to development passes through industrialisation, not necessarily with the objective of building factories and producing goods alone but because it is a step in changing productive systems and modernising the economic ecosystem.

This book goes beyond the happy narrative about 'the rise of Africa' and attempts to move the debates from rhetoric to reality. It offers innovative policy perspectives on critical issues and actions necessary for change in the complex context of African economies, while focusing on long-term development.

The book is constructed around challenges, no less than eight of them. Like sailors that face daunting waves and learn through experience how to be better prepared, Africans need to rise to a multitude of challenges with determination. The learning is in the journey. To make an object we start with the raw materials. To transform Africa, we have to start with what is there. If it is rough, difficult, let us double the energy. Smooth seas do not make skilful sailors.

CONTENTS

CHAPTER 1

Introduction: Reflecting on Africa's Contemporary Dynamics

The last decade and a half has seen African economies register an increase of growth of about 5%—thanks to factors such as improved economic governance and macroeconomic management, increased internal consumption, and the rise in the demand and prices for a considerable number of commodities. The net gross domestic product (GDP) growth is expected to continue its upward trajectory, even though in the last few years, fragility in terms of growth has been observed when Africa moved south like many other parts of the world (AfDB et al. 2016). The worrying pattern is the tendency of the continent to grow rapidly yet transform slowly, making it vulnerable to headwinds! To sustain the positive socio-economic outcomes from the recent growth, African countries must revisit the current development models and reap benefits that may result from real structural transformation.

African leaders are committed to a forward-looking vision for 50 years, following the adoption of Agenda 2063 by the African Union (AU). This agenda was first sketched during the jubilee celebrations of the organisation in Addis Ababa in May 2013, and subsequently, it was adopted by a Heads of State Summit in January 2015, followed by the approval of its First Ten-Year Implementation Plan (FTYIP) in June of the same year in a follow-up Summit in Sandton, South Africa. Africa, like the entire membership of the United Nations, is committed to the implementation of the so-called Sustainable Development Goals or Agenda 2030—a blueprint devised to address the economic, social, and environmental challenges of

C. Lopes, *Africa in Transformation*,
https://doi.org/10.1007/978-3-030-01291-5_1

1

our planet. These combined aspirations are quite ambitious. They comprise the political proclamations that must be followed while bringing about practical policy changes, which, in turn, point in the direction of structural transformation.

Economic growth, on its own, has been insufficient for transforming Africa. Despite its vast natural and human resources, poverty and inequality have continued to persist while prompting some commentators to ask whether this resource curse defines the continent (The Economist 2015). The externally driven commodity demand fails to generate economy-wide spill-over effects at the national and regional levels. The manufacturing industry still accounts for only a meagre share of the net GDP. The region—particularly the countries emerging out of conflict—must, therefore, prioritise social, economic, and political inclusion, as these are the pillars necessary for holding together a progressive, inclusive society. A sustained and inclusive economic growth is possible with the implementation of appropriate policies developed to create and distribute wealth as well as address inequalities at the continent level. However, such an agenda will be inadequate to catapult Africa into a more energised path if it remains in the realm of theory or is poorly executed. For that to happen, it is argued that there is a need to challenge the characteristics of the current development model.

To translate rapid economic growth into sustained and inclusive development, countries must be encouraged to put in place strategies that foster economic diversification, create jobs, reduce inequality, and boost access to basic services. Policies must also address spatial inequalities (differences between urban and rural areas and across regions) along with low intergenerational mobility in areas such as education, health, and employment that are plagued with inequality. However, eradicating poverty through hard and well-planned work requires the ability of people to sustain themselves through good jobs. Additionally, an enhancement of the capacity and productivity of low-skilled occupations (which, for Africa, typically belongs in the rural agricultural activities) is also required. International Labour Organization (ILO) estimates that nearly US $10 trillion, in income transfers and associated social protection, is needed to eradicate extreme and moderate poverty by 2030—and, hence, the need for concerted efforts to radically change the approaches currently in vogue.

As a recap, Rick Rowden (2013) in an article for *Foreign Policy* that made the rounds rebukes Africans for tripping over themselves in their bursting eagerness to promote the 'Africa rising' narrative. He argues that the underpinning data and indicators forward a bleak picture. Africans typically look at high GDP growth rates, rising per capita incomes, and the explosive growth of smartphones or mobile banking as evidence that Africa is 'developing'. He argues as follows:

> these indicators only give a partial picture of how well development is going—at least as the term has been understood over the last few centuries. From late 15th century England, all the way up to the East Asian Tigers of recent renown, development has generally been taken as a synonym for 'industrialization'. Rich countries figured out long ago, if economies are not moving out of dead-end activities that only provide diminishing returns over time (primary agriculture and extractive activities such as mining, logging, and fisheries), and into activities that provide increasing returns over time (manufacturing and services), then you can't really say they are developing. (Rowden 2013)

Rowden is right to a point. It is true that, in general, African data is not the most reliable. However, in most cases, this is because outdated methodologies and samples are employed for data procurement, not to mention the absence of closest-to-real data points. The process is guided by under-estimations, rather than by the generalisability potential. This further validates the argument that what we are observing is not the kind of transformation Africa should aspire towards.

Despite progress in human development indicators, such as universal access to primary education or drastic reductions in mother and child mortality, I am convinced that the current inability to address a number of transformational challenges is still trapping the continent into a state of low equilibrium, and, these self-same challenges are the focus of this book. It is critical to laboriously contextualise the key issues each time that may explain deceiving perceptions of pessimism and negativity. This book elects eight challenges that could contribute to a better reading of current transformation challenges.

THE MAP OF THIS BOOK

Narratives about Africa tend to be deceiving due to poor data and evidence, historical negative perceptions, and simplistic and superficial views, often linked to lack of comparative studies with other regions of the world.

It is as if Africa was an isolated entity geographically but also historically. This type of exceptionalism has been to the detriment of the continent's image.

It is against this background that I have decided to present some of the challenges I consider the most prominent. It is a personal choice established around eight challenges—changing politics, respecting diversity, understanding policy space, structurally transforming through industrialisation, increasing agricultural productivity, revisiting the social contract, adjusting to climate change, and inserting agency in the relations with China—that this book seeks to delve into.

I review some of the pressing development challenges facing African countries while providing my contribution to optimum remedies to existing problems with suggestions on how to make the best of what is available. I also outline some of the conditions for a desperately needed space to adopt industrial policies beyond the happy narrative about 'the rise of Africa'.

The choice of the challenges is, to some extent, arbitrary. Certainly, many important megatrends affecting Africa could have been the subject of specific additional chapters, such as the demographic changes and the related human mobility, the role of capacity for development, technology and innovation impacts, or implications resulting from accelerated urbanisation. I believe, nevertheless, that the intertwined nature of the challenges requires a choice, for the sake of clarity.

I consider that for change to happen, the continent must resolve political issues. This includes the most important political challenge in Africa, which is related to the respect for diversity. I have tried to diagnose in Chap. 2 current African political trends and squarely address the controversies surrounding the interpretations of democracy and the influence of external agents in the domestic developments in most countries. That is the starting point of my argument.

Most countries in Africa have limited capacities to undertake the wide range of measures required for a smooth transition from conflict to a path of peace, stability, and good governance—all of which are the chief ingredients of inclusive sustainable development. There seems to be a mythical dilemma revolving around which direction the continent should steer towards—constitutionalism, democracy, or development? Obviously, these three big 'ticket' items are not rivals, and they can, certainly, be achieved in complementarity to each other. However, there are some pertinent questions that need to be asked—such as, does holding regular election equate to democracy, or can a larger debate on the pitfalls of constitutional debates in Africa help address some of the difficult links between rhetoric and reality? I would like to agree with Daron Acemoglu and his colleague that development, constitutionalism, and democracy are self-reinforcing (see Acemoglu and Robinson 2012). Agreeing to such principles does not necessarily facilitate the task of interpreting the complexities associated with the path to build sustainable democratic societies.

The world is observing the limits of representational democracy and the faith in parties as the pillars of political competitive processes. The emergence of social media activism and contestation of elected powers with massive popular mobilisation have shaken stable democracies and opened the possibility for populism to take root. Africans are not immune to such debates. In countries as far apart as Tunisia, Niger, Egypt, Togo, Gambia, Mozambique, Burkina Faso, or the Democratic Republic of Congo, popular uprisings oblige constitutional powers to retreat and make concessions that were difficult to consider just few years back. Integrity of elections and electronic electoral systems are at the heart of new forms of dispute.

The discussion about the nature of Africa's transformation is becoming polarised between two interpretations of political systems. In the past such polarisation was between liberal and socialist prints, we then divided countries between liberal and democratic or dictatorships, whereas today the tendency is to divide between developmental states with an authoritarian bend versus open democracies that, unfortunately, often produce neo-patrimonial or rent-seeking elites. Africans are constantly interrogated about whether they prefer development or democracy to come first.

The book does not solve or even attempt to explain in detail these dilemmas. The purpose is rather to include the assessment of the political dimensions as part of any effort to understand transformation challenges. Politics, and the associated notion of leadership or personalisation of power, is definitely a major factor shaping Arica's future.

In 2015, I was invited to give the 13th annual lecture honouring Harold Wolpe. The lecture was scheduled at a time when his contribution to diagnosing Apartheid and its longer-term impact had started receiving more appreciation than before. Although Wolpe's writings focussed on South Africa, his provocative contributions surpassed the region it addressed. Wolpe was one of the admired 'conceptualisers' of his generation. By inventing a new radicalism, he left his mark on South African scholarship, introduced innovative approaches to the race question, and infuriated enough people to be classified by some as a pariah, and this radical approach to the race question inspires most of the arguments focusing on social identity in Chap. 2.

In a previous Wolpe lecture, Thandika Mkandawire (2007) argued that because of the failure of African nationalism—that is defined on its own terms—and due to the dominance of mystification in official historiography, there came about the introduction of refreshing new literature deconstructing and demystifying nationalist struggles. Unfortunately, recent accounts of nationalism still do not adequately capture the complexities of the post-colonial history of nationalism. Part of the problem stems from either the conflation of the two questions (national and social) or, simply, a preference for answering only one of them and eluding the one deemed uninteresting. In much of this literature, nationalist movements are discussed in terms of what they were or signified, rather than what they were not and what they did not signify, for whatever reasons.

One can extend the argument that colonialism itself, along with subsequent nationalist fervours, was always underpinned by economic undercurrents. In a sense, the nationalist project failed to bring forth an economy that is diversified and dominated by non-commodity, and this frustrated many political positions. Indeed, the argument in favour of structural transformation is made more pressing by the reality that post-colonial Africa is yet to alter the structure that has perpetually confined the continent as a supplier of raw materials to the industrialised West and now China.

Wolpe redefined how we need to diagnose African politics, but as correctly noted by Mkandawire, through his activism against Apartheid, Wolpe wanted us mostly to revisit the national and the social question, including what it means to live in a democracy. The national question has always been closely associated with the history of the oppressed or the colonised peoples. For much of the twentieth century, the national question first involved simply asserting one's humanity or the *présence africaine* as the title of the main outlet of Negritude-writing suggested; second, the acquisition of independence was incorporated; and third, the question was made to include aspects such as maintaining the unity and territorial integrity of the new state, as is evident in post-Apartheid South Africa, where the rhetoric was forwarded around achieving freedom as opposed to independence.

National identity, whether based on ethnicity or not, always contains a territorial component. The problem being simply 'how to hold the country together' (Wallerstein 1961: 95). The crisis concerning nation-building, which afflicted many countries in the continent, demonstrated the fallacy located in the central premise of African nationalism—that national independence could be achieved within the confines of the colonial delimited territory. Much attention should have been paid to the social question, given the problems engendered by social differentiation along the categorisations of class, ethnicity, gender as well as other social cleavages that arise or are unresolved within a nation. The reality is that Africa needs a new type of politics, advocated by people like Wolpe, whereby democratic principles guide our daily lives and the intricacies of this reformed and needed African politics are what Chap. 2 analyses in detail.

Chapter 3 finds its roots in yet another lecture I gave in honour of another thinker of African development challenges, Dr Jakes Gerwel. He was a principled man with the courage to match his actions with his noble ideals. While facing the challenges of his time in so small a way, he wrote a wonderful chapter on the history of the new South Africa. We are reminded of his assertiveness in wanting to ensure that all Africans, regardless of race and ethnicity, would have an opportunity to receive education. He believed it was important not only to understand the world but also to change it. It reminds me of similar public intellectuals, such as Edward Said, Frantz Fanon, or Amílcar Cabral, who placed enormous importance upon the contextualisation of liberation and freedom struggles through knowledge, culture, and education.

Gerwel's call for 'clear understanding, and profound understanding' mirrors the same deep understanding of the importance of making Africa better, not just freer. The importance of identity in defining how Africa shapes its development priorities is back on the table, and it must be resolved sooner rather than later. Gerwel was a towering South African as well as a global intellectual who reflected on these issues, and unsurprisingly, he was invited to give the inaugural Harold Wolpe memorial lecture in 2002. His pioneering doctoral thesis of 1979 treated the issues of identity by describing the way in which ideas that came forth in Afrikaner novels—from the period of 1875–1948—became agents for the racial attitudes that climaxed during the Apartheid state era.

I try to address the issue of diversity, a cornerstone of Africa's democratic experiments, with candour. The way countries deal with diversity has gotten worse with the introduction of the 'winner-takes-all' approach. In many countries winners use the legitimacy of the vote to smash minorities, treated as enemies, not just opponents. There is a deliberate attempt to eliminate alternative identities to the one proclaimed as national. Indeed, the identity question continues to hound Africa.

Why is this so? Several historical factors explain such behaviour.

Authors such as Ali Mazrui (1986), Mahmood Mamdani (1996), Brian Raftopoulos (1999), and Alois Mlambo (2001, 2013) have followed Gerwel in the quest to tease out the processes of identity-making and state-building in a multiethnic and multiracial society—processes that emerge from a protracted armed struggle against racially ordered, settler-colonial domination. It is important to examine the extent to which historical factors, such as the nature of the state, the prevailing national political economy, and regional and international forces and developments, have shaped notions of the sense of belonging and citizenship over time and have affected state-building and development efforts.

Other authors, such as Amartya Sen (2007) and Kwame Anthony Appiah (2015), have brilliantly demonstrated the need for us to embrace identities as a sophisticated demonstration of human behaviour, not as a zero-sum game. Each individual can embrace as many identities as its life experience absorbed and make feel comfortable. Institutions deriving from more restricted interpretations of common culture tend to see these expressions of freedom with fear. More so if entire communities maintain solid references and want to keep them for their own self-preservation.

According to Sen 'When we shift our attitudes from the notion of being identical to oneself to that of sharing an identity with others of a particular group (which is the form the idea of social identity very often takes) the complexity increases further. Indeed, many contemporary political and social issues revolve around conflicting claims of disparate identities nurturing diverse groups, since the conception of identity influences, in many different ways, or thoughts and actions' (Sen 2007: xii).

Often nationalist attitudes tend to brush aside collective expressions and often manifest intolerance to multiplicity of identities through political repression or open conflict.

Africa is plagued with leaders feeling threatened by diversity and using ethnicity, or other forms of finger-pointing group behaviour, to castigate vulnerable or marginalised groups. For instance, xenophobic attacks against migrants within the continent are a recurrent demonstration of the limits of pan-African ideology when it comes to the respect of other fellow

Africans as belonging to one united Africa. But more importantly these developments permeate the internal political debates in ways that put to shame Africans criticism of other non-African countries attitudes towards African migrants.

The struggle to create stable and inclusive societies in Africa cannot ignore the poor record of African political institutions regarding diversity and identity. Chapter 3 identifies this challenge as essential for transformation.

Understanding the debates that address intricacies of identities helps in contextualising the development path that most Africans followed, either by choice or due to imposition. Many would argue it was an 'imposed choice'. That could explain why there is a tendency to externalise the justifications for all that goes bad, not accepting culpability, and, in the process, forgo needed accountability. That is the core of the argument in Chap. 4.

In the 1980s and 1990s, 'getting prices right' and rolling back the state were recommended by the Washington Consensus as being conditions essential for the transformation and development of Africa and the rest of the developing world (see earlier critiques on the state as inhibitor of development in Krueger 1974). The stylised facts of the Structural Adjustment periods of the 1980s and 1990s showed how haemorrhaged African economies were. Public service delivery and associated quality had declined. Many began to wonder whether the market mechanism alone could do the trick, as preached by the Washington-based Bretton Woods institutions. Attempts emerged to bring the state back in and to reinvigorate planning as well as give nuance to the more simplistic liberalisation precepts. Somehow, growth returned and, with it, claims about whose success it was.

The debate about a return to Keynesian approaches emerged, generating policy space for revisiting Africa's experience with structural adjustment programmes. I examine this issue in Chap. 4. The discussion about a post-Washington Consensus had, until recently, many elements cutting across a wide range of macroeconomic policies. There is now a questioning of the extent to which the innovative approaches were executed. Changes in major economies question liberalisation and globalisation from a different angle. In Washington, a new wave promoting protectionist instincts makes the word 'consensus' difficult to be applied to any policy position.

While paying necessary attention to processes at the international level, African states need to incorporate regional and transboundary cooperation and partnerships into their policymaking and implementation processes. Regional integration, including, for example, the provision of first-rate infrastructure, is imperative for Africa to overcome the limitations constraining small national economies and to enhance intra-Africa trade. International trends also impact on the governance and other drivers of development, particularly through global negotiations such as those on trade and climate change. Indeed, as the world moves towards a 'green economy', Africa faces the challenge of balancing its desire for fast growth along conventional lines with the need to adapt to climate change and develop along more environmentally sustainable lines.

Democracy and the rule of law provide the necessary linkages through which the bureaucracy can interact with all key stakeholders, including the private sector and civil society organisations. In this context, the design and implementation of plans and policies should comprehend monitoring and evaluation mechanisms, assessment and reviewing of plans and policies under implementation, with broad stakeholder participation and involvement. The emerging post-Washington Consensus, in so far as Africa is concerned, ought to be about addressing growth with inequality, or how future growth must be equitably shared. By revisiting what must change, one realises how complex the novel approach will have to be, not tolerating complacent narratives about the continent.

The good news though is that the main actors that created and were defending the Washington Consensus have themselves moved on, not necessarily all in the same direction though. The Bretton Woods institutions have distanced themselves from the advice that was the fulcrum of their engagements in the 1980s and 1990s. Actors like the United States have been more erratic and ambiguous. The Organisation for Economic Co-operation and Development (OECD) as an organisation has adhered to several quasi-Keynesian views, particularly in regard to the role of the state.

One good example about the robustness of the discussion is the controversy around the Special Drawing Rights (SDR). The International Monetary Fund (IMF) now accepts that there is a need for 'reducing the extent and costs of international reserve accumulation; augmenting the supply of safe global assets and facilitating diversification; and reducing the impact of exchange rate volatility among major currencies. Expanding the SDR basket to major emerging market currencies presents trade-offs, but could further support these objectives' (IMF 2011). This represents an important geopolitical shift.

Another important demonstration of flexibility is the introduction of more flexible criteria for assessing performance through an evolving IMF conditionality framework (IMF 2017b). Closer to the interests of the majority of African countries the debt sustainability criteria for low-income countries have also been made more malleable (IMF 2017a).

The 2017 spring meetings of the IMF and World Bank centred on the issue of inequality, something unsung just a few years back. Authors such as Angus Deaton and Thomas Piketty have become 'must quote' in the references of institutional players that used to believe markets would correct imbalances on their own. Articles published by IMF and World Bank researchers cuddle non-governmental organisation (NGO) language and justify policy on the basis of the United Nations Agenda 2030.

These developments increase policy space and democratise a debate that has been marked by aggressive defence of orthodox views. Chapter 4 explores how African players can use such openness to their benefit.

Chapter 5 implores Africans to appreciate the undertones of the 'Africa rising' narrative. This narrative has been driven by the view that new profitable opportunities exist in Africa. The objective of this narrative was not Africa-centred. Africa needs its own narrative, where its countries revisit the current development models and reap benefits that result from their structural transformation processes. Africans should measure whether their productive structures are changing or not. The unfortunate reality is that many African economies do not have the strategies or the determination that is necessary for driving a successful economic structural transformation. As a result, limited change has rendered made many African countries vulnerable to inherent fluctuations of the international commodity markets, leading to significant growth volatility. This vulnerability to external shocks is due to several interacting factors linked to the 'absence' of a developmental state. Dependence on commodity trade in the face of natural resource abundance demands that more focus be given to value-addition across all production processes and nodes. Africa must prioritise industrialisation to speed up the development of various value-addition activities.

The premises for discussing structural transformation dates back to the literature of 1950s (Lopes et al. 2017) and gained prominence with the dualistic model presented by Nobel Prize winner Arthur Lewis (1955).

Lewis demonstrated that when labour shifts from agriculture into manufacturing there is increased output and productivity in the economy. Failures of neo-classic economic models have resuscitated the need for more attention to be given to the imperatives of structural economic transformation on the African context. The shift from lower to higher productivity is normally made possible by accelerated industrialisation. Although Africa has not totally bypassed this trend, evidence available and the literature are quite consensual about the very negligible role manufacturing value-addition has played in the economies. With a spectacular growth of its workforce the need for jobs is quite urgent. Without industrialisation it will be difficult to imagine how Africa can respond to the challenge.

In Chap. 5 I review how the debate about structural transformation is being shaped and the vital role industrialisation plays in it. The question I seek to answer in this chapter is, what should be the nature of the transformative industrial policies for Africa?

We all acknowledge that African countries have a real opportunity to capitalise on their resource endowments and high international commodity prices as well as on opportunities from the changes in the global economy to promote economic transformation through industrialisation, which would, in turn, address poverty, inequality, and unemployment. If grasped, these opportunities will help Africa promote competitiveness, reduce its dependence on primary commodity exports and associated vulnerability to shocks, and emerge as a new global growth pole. The question is not whether Africa can industrialise by ignoring its commodities and other resources, but rather how it can use them for value-addition, the introduction of new services, and enhancement of technological capabilities. This may not apply to all African countries, and this should not be the only way African resource-rich countries industrialise.

Making the most of Africa's diverse resources requires appropriate development-planning frameworks and effective industrial policies that are evidence-based and consider what influences can establish a link between breadth and depth as well as the structural and country-specific drivers (see Lopes et al. 2017; ECA 2013a, 2014a, 2015, 2016 push this line of arguments).

In Chap. 6, I examine the importance of agriculture in Africa's effort to transform and industrialise. I argue that one of the pillars and, indeed, a driving force behind Africa's structural transformation derives its strength from the agricultural sector. Evidence suggests that countries across the globe that have increased productivity have benefitted from economic growth that is sustained through agricultural transformation. Africans have an opportunity, now more than ever before, to change their lives through increased and enhanced agri-business that connects smallholders to national, regional, and global value chains.

In the past food security has been given rightful prominence in the aid and development programmes, given the poverty-reduction focus. There is now realisation such laudable focus cannot be a replacement for real transformation. Treating the primary sector from a social protection angle has not contributed to uplift the majority of those dependent on these activities for their insertion in the economy. As a result, the percentage of the primary sector in general, and agriculture in particular, for the GDP of almost all African countries has been diminishing considerably. On average the importance of services has surpassed the importance of agriculture.

It is important to renew the building blocks that are necessary for a deeper discussion on the connection to be made between agriculture and industrialisation. Often the focus on agriculture has been disassociated from industrialisation. Successful green revolutions were based on significant productivity gains obtained precisely because of the pull factor of more modern systems of production. Labour contributions have been important. Infrastructure and backward and forward value chains linkages were crucial. Countries that introduce specific quick wins through interventionist policies are assessed in Chap. 6. The chapter addresses the major obstacles hampering Africa's agricultural transformation through examples based on field research conducted by the Economic Commission for Africa (ECA) (ECA 2013a, b, c, 2014a, b). The challenges for the primary sector go beyond what some official documents like the Comprehensive Africa Agriculture Development Programme (CAADP) proposes (NEPAD 2010). There is a need for a strategy that considers the fact that opportunities specifically African need to consider the stages at which other developing regions are.

Indeed, Africa's renewed development ambitions are occurring in a brave new world, where emergent dangers such as climate change and environmental destruction loom large. Clearly, climate change imposes upon us the importance of not doing business as usual. The technology and know-how now exist for Africa to take a green industrial pathway.

Chapter 7 discusses the importance of a 'green' development strategy and how it is consequential to pursue such path as a way of engaging on a new social contract. It starts by demonstrating that the evolution of the sustainability concept has its roots in Rousseau's notion of intergenerational solidarity. It is important to revisit the philosophical tenets that gave substance to the various formulations of sustainable development. I seek to resolve the tension between environmental concerns, resulting from global ecological consequences of human activities on one hand and economic, social, and political concerns on the other.

The central tenet of sustainable development resides in the concept of equity and social justice for all. The notion of sustainable development must be flexible and dynamic to accommodate ecological and social realities. Sustainable development, primarily, is a process of transformative change, but it occurs only in an enabling environment supported by robust institutions and a set of rules that must be adhered to. The challenge of a multilateral governance relates to the issues of governing the 'commons' based on set global agendas, legitimate principle of common actions, and a bringing together of global communities to commit to a process of implementing change at the local, national, and international levels. There must be coordinated state actions to materialise the dream of green economy and development into reality, including bypassing the so-called Kuznets curve (see Kuznets 1955, for seminal idea).

In the African context the challenge of a new social contract resides mostly on balancing environmental and demographic concerns in the structural transformation process. The contemporary interpretation of a social contract in any part of the world cannot ignore the demographic tectonic shifts that will define most of the early part of the twenty-first century. Africa has already the youngest population average of any continent and that record will be enhanced between now and mid-century. Many would be worried about the size of this youth bulge in terms of economic opportunities and environmental stress. Yet one has also to bear in mind the rest of the world will be ageing, OECD countries in particular. This presents challenges of completely different order, not least to expect intergenerational solidarity when the older generation is not leaving in the same territorial space as the younger generation.

The acceleration of digital opportunities and computer-led technological developments will increase the pressure for new forms of social contract. Artificial intelligence, genomics, and 3D printing will be added to the knowledge-intensive capacities already being deployed through automation and robotisation. As a latecomer Africa will have a much more difficult adaptation aptitude and can suffer from technological and innovation systems enshrined in the current intellectual property regimes.

Chapter 8 delves deeper into making a convincing case for the centrality of climate change in the efforts of Africa's policymakers. In this chapter I argue that climate change will present us with a wide range of issues, including the need for African countries to refocus their attention to end hunger, achieve food security and improved nutrition, and promote sustainable agriculture. These go hand in hand with combating climate change and its impacts through climate smart agriculture (CSA) and green industrialisation (Brahmbhatt et al. 2017; ECA 2016; AfDB et al. 2013). Climate change mitigation and adaptation will also assume importance in this context.

This chapter draws on my push for a more strategic positioning of the African negotiators during an African Sustainable Development Forum that took place in Addis Ababa in 2015. The strategy influenced many policies designed for implementation across the continent. Subsequently, I have been advocating for a closer link between industrialisation efforts and climate change opportunities. This could be achieved through sustained robust economic growth. I argue that implement pricing and regulatory and public investment policies can offset market failures and foster development of domestic green markets. There is a need also to strengthen industrial development policies and increasingly exploit global green market opportunities. And finally, attention should be devoted to policies that strengthen capacity and entrepreneurship, including green entrepreneurship, by adopting unique strategies for the three major types of firms in Africa's industrial sector.

In the international negotiations arena Africans have been demonstrating a renewed agency to defend outcomes more favourable to them. This chapter tries to present some progress and shortcomings in that regard.

The other important challenge that I discuss in Chap. 8 is the lack of attention, if not total neglect, on the importance of the so-called blue economy. The time is now for us to think about how marine resources could better contribute to Africa's economy.

I might be stating the obvious here, but if you think of Africa as a big island, the water body of which is three times larger than its land mass, the importance of its oceans and seas cannot be understated. This was somehow recognised by Africa's leaders when they adopted an Integrated Maritime Strategy (2050 AIM Strategy) at an AU Summit in Addis Ababa in 2014, followed by a themed Maritime Summit held in Togo in October 2016. All water bodies, including lakes, rivers, and underground water in addition to seas and the coast, are unique resources that are mostly neglected and often forgotten. The largest sectors of the current African aquatic and ocean-based economy are fisheries, aquaculture, tourism, transport, ports, coastal mining, and energy. Additionally, the blue economy approach that emphasises upon interconnectedness with other sectors is responsive to emerging and frontier sectors and supports important social considerations, such as gender mainstreaming, food and water security, poverty alleviation, wealth retention, and job creation. The blue economy can, thus, play a significant role in Africa's structural transformation.

I had to include in the book some aspects of the African relationship with the rest of the world. Chapter 9 could have been about the challenges of Africa's relationships. However, I decided to focus on the China relationship in particular, given its size and significance.

The continent needs partnerships for fast implementation (particularly in the areas of financial resources, trade, investments, and capacity-building) of its development priorities. Africa's funding needs outstrip its domestic resource capabilities—due to low domestic savings, shallow capital markets, weak financial intermediation, large informal sector, illicit transfer of funds, and fiscal management, and governance challenges.

While considering potential efficiency gains, Africa would still face an infrastructure funding gap of around US $90 billion per year, mainly because of the increasing energy requirements (AfDB et al. 2015).

One of the most contested issues in the current assessments of African development trajectory is the emergence of new partners such as China, which is redefining how the continent engages with the rest of the world. The Second Forum on China-Africa Cooperation Summit, held in Johannesburg in December 2015, demonstrated the extent of the changes in China's relationship with Africa (see e.g. Shelton et al. 2015). China's tripling of its financing commitment, amounting to a funding of US $60 billion for the period 2015–2017, signalled its confidence in the economic transformation prospects of the African continent. I would like to argue that the changing Sino-African relationship is underpinned by a shift towards a more balanced partnership that recognises Africa's socio-economic and political priorities beyond the demand for its natural resources.

There is need to unpack the different dimensions of the links between Africa and China, including the 'untold story' of the relationship, which is the growing interest of Africa in the Chinese economy. Chapter 9 discusses the importance of reinserting African agency in Sino-African relations. Africa must make the best of its relations with the Chinese.

To close, the 'rise of Africa' narrative borrowed immensely from a simplistic view of commodities being central for the stimulation of the continent's economic activity; yet, today, the largest contributor to growth is internal consumption and the largest sector is the services. Such facts on their own show the scale of misperceptions and the long road to travel. Any attempt at comprehensiveness would have been overambitious. This book, unsurprisingly, makes a modest attempt to just illustrate the complexity of observed transitions in the continent through examples that are more commonly debated. A set of key policy recommendations wrap up the effort in a concluding chapter (Chap. 10).

REFERENCES

Acemoglu, D., & Robinson, J. (2012). *Why Nations Fail: The Origins of Power, Prosperity, and Poverty*. New York: Crown Publishers.

AfDB, OECD, & UNDP. (2013). Structural Transformation and Natural Resources. *African Economic Outlook*. Paris: OECD Publishing.

AfDB, OECD, & UNDP. (2015). Regional Development and Spatial Inclusion. *African Economic Outlook*. Paris: OECD Publishing.

AfDB, OECD, & UNDP. (2016). Sustainable Cities and Structural Transformation. *African Economic Outlook*. Paris: OECD Publishing.

Appiah, K. A. (2015). *Cosmopolitanism: Ethics in a World of Strangers*. London: Penguin.

Brahmbhatt, M., Haddaoui, C., & Page, J. (2017). *Green Industrialisation and Entrepreneurship in Africa*. NCE Working Paper, Washington, DC.

ECA. (2013a). *Millennium Development Goals Report 2013: Assessing Progress in Africa Towards the Millennium Development Goals Food Security in Africa – Issues, Challenges and Lessons*. Addis Ababa: ECA.

ECA. (2013b). *Rethinking Agricultural and Rural Transformation in Africa. Challenges, Opportunities and Strategic Policy Options*. Addis Ababa: ECA, Mimeo.

ECA. (2013c). *Status of Food Security in Africa: A Parliamentary Document*. Addis Ababa: ECA.

ECA. (2014a). *Economic Report for Africa: Dynamic Industrial Policy in Africa*. Addis Ababa: ECA.

ECA. (2014b). *Rethinking Agricultural and Rural Transformation in Africa – The Necessary Conditions for Success: The Case of Mauritius*. Addis Ababa: ECA.

ECA. (2015). *Economic Report on Africa: Industrializing Through Trade.* Addis Ababa: ECA.

ECA. (2016). *Transformative Industrial Policy for Africa.* Addis Ababa: ECA.

The Economist. (2015, January 8). African Economic Growth – The Twilight of the Resource Curse? *The Economist.* Retrieved July 16, 2015, from http://www.economist.com/news/middle-east-and-africa/21638141-africas-growth-being-powered-things-other-commodities-twilight.

IMF. (2011). *Enhancing International Monetary Stability – A Role for the SDR?* Retrieved January 23, 2011, from https://www.imf.org/external/np/pp/eng/2011/010711.pdf.

IMF. (2017a). *Debt Sustainability Framework for Low-Income Countries.* Retrieved October 20, 2017, from https://www.imf.org/external/pubs/ft/dsa/lic.htm.

IMF. (2017b). *IMF Conditionality.* Retrieved October 20, 2017, from http://www.imf.org/en/About/Factsheets/Sheets/2016/08/02/21/28/IMF-Conditionality.

Krueger, A. (1974). The Political Economy of a Rent Seeking Society. *American Economic Review, 64*(94), 291–303.

Kuznets, S. (1955). Economic Growth and Income Inequality. *American Economic Review, 49*(1), 1–28.

Lewis, A. (1955). *The Theory of Economic Growth.* Chicago: R. D. Irwin.

Lopes, C., Hamdock, A., & Elhiraika, A. (Eds.). (2017). *Macroeconomic Policy Framework for Africa's Structural Transformation.* London: Palgrave Macmillan.

Mamdani, M. (1996). *Citizen and Subject: Contemporary Africa and the Legacy of Late Colonialism.* Princeton, NJ: Princeton University Press.

Mazrui, A. (1986). *The Africans: A Triple Heritage.* New York: Little Brown & Co.

Mkandawire, T. (2007). *From the National Question to the Social Question.* 5th Harold Wolpe Memorial Lecture Online. Retrieved June 14, 2014, from http://www.wolpetrust.org.za/lectures/2007/National%20Question_Social%20Question.pdf.

Mlambo, A. S. (2001). "Some Are More White Than Others": Racial Chauvinism as a Factor in Rhodesian Immigration Policy, 1890 to 1963. *Zambezia, 27*(2), 139–160.

Mlambo, A. S. (2013). Becoming Zimbabwe or Becoming Zimbabwean: Identity, Nationalism and State-Building. *Africa Spectrum, 48*(1), 49–70.

NEPAD. (2010). *Accelerating CAADP Country Implementation.* Midrand: NEPAD.

Raftopoulos, B. (1999). Problematising Nationalism in Zimbabwe: A Historiographical Review. *Zambezia, 26*(2), 115–134.

Rowden, R. (2013, January 4). The Myth of Africa's Rise: Why the Rumors of Africa's Explosive Growth Have Been Greatly Exaggerated. *Foreign Policy*. Retrieved July 13, 2013, from http://foreignpolicy.com/2013/01/04/the-myth-of-africas-rise/.
Sen, A. (2007). *Identity and Violence*. New York: WW Norton.
Shelton, G., Funeka, Y. A., & Li, A. (Eds.). (2015). *FOCAC 2015 – A New Beginning of China-Africa Relations*. Pretoria: Africa Institute of South Africa.
Wallerstein, E. (1961). *The Politics of Independence*. New York: Vintage Books.

CHAPTER 2

Changing Politics

When I was ten, I saw a telephone for the first time. It was in my native place, Guinea Bissau, where modern-day innovations took time in getting introduced. My uncle—who lived in the same street as my family behind the only hotel in town called the Grande Hotel, although it only had 20 rooms—was a privileged fellow. He worked at the central post office as a senior staff and, therefore, could easily justify why he was one of the first ones to have a telephone. At those times, a telephone used to be one of those bulky thermo-plastic type of machines, with a rotary circle for dialling. It had ten digits, but in fact, only '0' worked. It served to call the operator who established the connection manually.

I marvelled upon the fact that one could talk without seeing and could be heard from afar without shouting across. In my innocence, I could not relate that instrument with anything but pure joy. However, soon after, my father was put in jail by the Portuguese Intelligence police (PIDE) because of his links with terrorism, as I was told. This was disturbing news. I still remember that the telephone was, indeed, associated with pure joy, because much later, it was through it that we were informed that he was doing fine, but no more than that bare minimum could be conveyed to us.

The telephony revolution—in fact, the communication revolution—is closely associated with how African politics plays out in the current scenario. I have, in one generation, moved from basic telephone and devices to a hand-held powerful computer with a speed that did not have an equivalent of what had been experienced by all the previous generations.

© The Author(s) 2019
C. Lopes, *Africa in Transformation*,
https://doi.org/10.1007/978-3-030-01291-5_2

And this revolution is happening in Africa, in comparative terms, faster than in any other region in the world.

Discussing voice, identity, and expression of will to exercise power is now completely different from what has been undertaken before—thanks to the fact that the six billion cell phones available in the world are making us one big family. Families have both good and bad behaviours; they enshrine the complexity of the human fabric with its contradictions, assumptions, and conquests. Families aspire to achieve harmony, but by no means can they automatically acquire it. Therefore, they manage their behaviour with beliefs, protocols, and acquired habits—in one word, they regulate.

Undercurrents and Trends

It is said that the most sophisticated form of regulation is democracy. Let us assess the African record in this regard. The trend towards democratic politics in Africa, as elsewhere in the world, has become ubiquitous. Democracy, however imperfect it may be, has assumed a capital position in town, defining the basis of politics and power as well as a means for determining values in political communities. African politics, in both its historical and contemporary dimensions, as Naomi Chazan et al. rightly noted, 'constitute the microcosm of political forms and contents, experiences and patterns, trends and prospects' (1999: 6).

In their genealogy, countries' differing experiences and encounters have marked their democratic footprint. Political regimes, ranging from multiparty system to military dictatorships, one-party rule, political monarchies, and, sometimes, outright political autocracy and tyranny, have all existed in contemporary Africa.

Countries' records have differed in form and content. The configuration of class and social context, coalition building, alignment, and realignment of political actors, agencies, and political outcomes contributes to defying any strict characterisation of African politics. Indeed, some argue that in terms of politics, we should talk about 'Africas' and not 'Africa' in a monolithic sense.

There is no doubt that comprehending African politics in its historical and contemporary dimensions has kept African scholars busy. They have created narratives, conceptual and theoretical constructions, deconstructions and reconstructions, polemical and ideological debates, and intellectual projections and advocacy that are vast and sometimes overwhelming.

The range of the discourses includes dissecting the colonial encounter and its political economy, post-colonial nation-building, state-civil society relations, political transitions, social movements in the political process, gender, and politics, parties and other political institutions, and, more recently, the interface between democracy and the development of markets.

Allow me to capture and analyse some of the paradigms and perspectives necessary to diagnose changes occurring throughout the continent.

In diagnosing African politics, perspectives and paradigms have been adopted from different historical contexts. Serious intellectual debates were generated amongst African scholars and between them and the Africanists. These paradigms can be teased out in three broad categories. The first is what we refer to as the social identity paradigm; the second is the political economy paradigm; and the third is the social movement paradigm.

The first paradigm of social identity has different strands. Perhaps, a good starting point is the theory of the two publics articulated by Peter Ekeh (1975), which focus on how the colonial encounter shaped the nature of politics in Africa, through the bifurcation of individual identities, personalities, and public spaces. Colonialism, in Ekeh's view, was an 'epochal event whose supra-individual consequences have lingered in fundamental ways, long after actual colonisation and the colonial situation have ceased to exist. Colonialism is to Africa what the industrial revolution and French revolution were to Europe' (Osaghae 2003: 3). To elaborate, 'it is to the colonial experience that any valid conceptualisation of the unique nature of African politics must look' (Ekeh 1975: 93). According to Ekeh, the problem of corruption, mismanagement, personalisation of power, and political autocracy cannot be understood except through a sociological analysis of how the colonial experience reshaped social values through the kind of structures and institutions created, of which the conditions and realities subsist until the present.

Colonialism created dual public spaces and dual identities—what Ekeh referred to as the civic and the primordial publics. The civic public is an arena of political a-moralism, while the primordial public is the space for public morality and decency. Given the brutality and arbitrariness of colonial governance, the civic public space lacked legitimacy and public support; or in other words, it was an arena viewed by many with suspicion, antipathy, and possibly, as opportunity for plunder. The primordial space is that of traditional affection—where the people find comfort, acceptance, and a sense of belonging; hence, it confers legitimacy and moral values—a bit like the treatment we expect from being part of a family. As the state remains 'alien', people's perceptions and attitude towards it, including those of the people who manage state power, remain one of distrust, poor support, and, often, vandalism. The crisis of the state and politics in Africa is, therefore, located in this dualism of public spaces and the political construction of legitimacy.

When discussing the social identity paradigm, the ethnic dimension of politics becomes an important strand of African politics. Prominent scholars, including Onigu Otite (1990), Eghosa Osaghae (2001), Mahmood Mamdani (1996), and Archie Mafeje (1971, 1991), dwell on this issue extensively. Archie Mafeje provides a useful deconstruction of tribalism, which, hitherto, was used by Western anthropological researchers in their study of Africa—its politics and society.

Mahmood Mamdani (1996) offers a very insightful analysis of social identity politics and the character of the state in his seminal book, *Citizens and Subjects*. With the concept of decentralised despotism, Mamdani sought to deconstruct the structure and mechanics of the colonial state and how it shaped intergroup relations in Africa. Premised on the logic of indirect rule, the colonial state was a bifurcated state, which existed at two levels—the central and local state. The local state was the domain of the native authorities, and that was where the natives were to be shelved into their distinct neat containers and governed. Ethnic identities and rigidities were the hallmark of the native authority system; every native was defined within the context of a native authority. While civil law governed the central state, customary law was the legal framework for the native authority system. The former was the domain of rights and the racialised; the latter was one of tradition and customs and the ethnicised. But custom, in this case, as Mamdani (1996: 22) noted, was the language of force, masking the uncustomary powers of the native authorities. African politics now needs to address this bifurcation that marks its social identity paradigm.

The pejorative notion of tribalism, which is often used in the study of the 'other' or the 'natives' by anthropological Africanists, distorts Africa's political and social realities and reinforces stereotypes of inferiority and social backwardness. Tribalism denotes 'self-contained, autonomous communities, practicing subsistence economy with no, or limited, external trade' (Mafeje 1971: 257). More recently, ethnicity and ethnic relations replaced the notion of tribal communities in the discourse. Ethnic groups, according to Onigu Otite (1990: 17), are categories of people characterised by cultural criteria of symbols, including language, value systems, and normative behaviour, and it comprises those whose members are anchored in a territory. They are neither autarkic groups nor are they excluded from constant interactions and reconfiguration. The thrust of the ethnic interpretations of politics in Africa is that the colonial policy of divide and rule, based on the ethnic identities cemented by ethnic principles, deepened interethnic competition and exacerbated ethnic conflicts. Indeed, access to the state and its resources, either at the local or at the national level, can be based on ethnic arithmetic, and hence, the size, social positioning, and political leverage exercised by ethnic groups become a driving force of power dynamics in Africa. There is a cesspool of struggles among ethnic identities to capture the state or, at least, gain control of its instrumentalities.

The way this reality permeated the independent states is the subject of many research contributions, but there is no major controversy that can be observed in this regard. Basically, it is admitted that upon independence, the bifurcated colonial state was de-racialised, but not democratised. Democratisation upon independence became synonymous to de-racialisation of civil power, rather than de-tribalisation of the customary power. However, issues of race, tribal roots, and ethnicity should not be ignored.

Another important body of contributions diagnosing African politics is the mostly Marxist political economy approach, which informs the political economy paradigm outlined earlier. Scholars like Samir Amin (1976, 1978), Walter Rodney (1972), Claude Ake (1981), Bade Onimode (1988), Nzongola-Ntalaja (1987), Peter Anyang' Nyong'o (1989), and Dani Nabudere (1978) have adopted this approach. For them, the global economic system is the driving force in shaping the context and dynamics of politics in peripheral countries in general, and Africa in particular. Some of these scholars focus on what they term the logic of imperialism, while others put emphasis on internal class formation and its power consequences. Samir Amin (1990), for example, underscores the fact that we need to understand the nature of accumulation on a world scale within the global capitalist system and its inherent contradictions before we can unravel the nature of politics in a specific country to effectively appropriate the same to the global framework. African countries are not marginalised in terms of integration into the global capitalist system; rather, the pattern of their integration, which he calls 'mal-integration', is the prominent issue.

Finally, another group of scholars focused on the issue of social movements and popular forces, which inform the social movements' paradigm, including civil society movements. This approach seeks to understand politics and power from 'below' and the struggles of the people for improved governance. This approach has been used in both understanding the decolonisation process and the recent wave of democratisation that swept the continent in late 1980s and 1990s (on recent democratisation see, e.g. Mamdani 2005; Mamdani et al. 1988; Anyang' Nyong'o 1987).

The above perspectives and paradigms offer alternative analytical lenses, which are historical, nuanced, and rigorous. These approaches are in contradiction to the mainstream perspectives, notably the neo-patrimonial school, which celebrates the pathologies of African politics. It describes African politics as a haven of patron-client relations, characterised by corruption, cronyism, informalisation of political life, and disorderly rules and procedure (see Van de Walle 2007). Indeed, Africa is seen to work through an inverse logic of political disorder and chaos (Chabal and Daloz 1999). Its political elites are believed to be capricious and perverse, inclined towards a 'politics of the belly' (Bayart 1993)—a euphemism for lawlessness and corruption. In its very extreme form, neo-patrimonial theory creates a parallel between African cultural traits and the decadence of African politics. African culture and traditions are viewed as being regressive and permissive of immoral political behaviour or conduct.

As Thandika Mkandawire (2013: 5) notes, the neo-patrimonial theory, while describing the styles of the exercise of authority, the mannerisms of certain colourful political leaders, or the social practices associated with some states and the individuals occupying distinct positions within them, fails in advancing our knowledge or our understanding of the nature of politics, economy, and society in Africa.

Analysing African politics is a contested issue. African countries are marked by their diversity. This plurality affects how politics evolve. Ethnic, religious, linguistic, spatial, gender, and class dimensions all contribute to the creation of a complex picture. For example, the continent has about 2110 living languages, constituting about 30% of the world's total. With forced amalgamation, there was the indiscriminate drawing of political boundaries by the colonial authorities, lumping non-identical groups and communities together in the newly created states. Politics has been rendered fractured, disempowering for the majority, non-inclusive, and, at times, even violent. Civil society organisations, for example, in many instances, were ruthlessly suppressed and dissent was regarded as treason.

Constructing nation-states and promoting cohesive national politics by groups and communities without identical social and political history, cultural affinity, or social contiguity have been a major challenge.

The trend of politics and political regimes that unfolded in the continent since independence is obviously not monolithic. Some countries kept faith with multiparty democratic politics, although with a mostly dominant one-party-system in vogue, while others did not bother with appearances and maintained an official one-party system. After their independence many countries were shoved into a cycle of military coups and political dictatorships.

NATURE OF POLITICS

There were two major global and national currents that influenced the nature of politics in the African countries: the Cold War and the imperative of nation-building. The politics of the Cold War promoted ideological proxies and satellite states, especially in Africa. What mattered in those proxy countries were not so much the internal configuration of power and the desires of the polity but external allegiances. Political accountability and the citizens' voices in the arena of domestic politics were discounted. The imperative of nation-building, on the other hand, sought implementation in the unitary systems of government, as a means of containing and managing diversity. One-party rule leaders were convinced that to contain the fissiparous tendencies of Africa's plural societies, political unison in a one-party state will prove to be the magic wand. However, this was never to be.

There was a concentration and centralisation of power around political leaders or oligarchs. In many countries, political power was highly centralised and managed both institutionally and operationally. Ethnic identities were also well entrenched. While civil society continued to grow exponentially, paradoxically, the political space shrank remarkably. The struggle for space that could make allowance for political dissent or identity expression to flourish mostly finds one channel of venting—through ethnicity—and this marks the crux of the social movement paradigm of African politics.

The changes that took place since the late 1980s, with the eclipse of the Cold War, soon gained momentum in Africa. Authoritarian regimes gradually gave way to nascent democratic attempts, shifting the nature of the political debate. Elections, political parties, contestation, rights, institutional checks, and governance accountability are now common currencies in Africa. A rich literature has emerged on the democratisation process in the continent, from both theoretical and empirical dimensions, comparing regional experiences and country case-studies (see, e.g. Chole and Ibrahim 1995; Ake 2000; Lumumba-Kasongo 2005; Nzongola-Ntalaja and Lee 1997; Boafo-Arthur 2007; Murunga and Nasongo 2007; Adejumobi 2002). And these works inform the social movement paradigm.

Another extended paradigm of African politics is that of liberal democracy. Claude Ake (2000: 9–11) provided a refreshing theoretical interrogation of the liberal democracy paradigm that dominated views not only in Africa but also outside. Ake argued that liberal democracy is markedly different from democracy, even though it tends to share affinities with it, with features like consent of the governed, formal political equality, inalienable human rights, accountability of power to the governed, and the rule of law. However, they are not one and the same. Indeed, liberal democracy is a negation of the whole concept of democracy. Instead of sovereignty of the people, liberal democracy offers sovereignty of the law (Ake 2000: 10).

Adebayo Olukoshi takes a distinct perspective from Claude Ake's and argues that it is possible to see democracy and capitalism as different projects in the history of the modern world, without necessarily having any automatic or organic correlation. Persuasively, he contends that 'it is not capitalism that is inherently democratic; the hidden and open, sometimes bitter, struggles against repressive tendencies and instincts have been central to the production of some of the reforms that, today, are the hallmark of liberal democracy' (1998: 14). In other words, liberal democracy arose, not necessarily because of but despite capitalism, and the possibility of its reproduction in other societies, including African countries with less developed capitalist system, is, therefore, possible as well as desirable.

Speaking of development in the context of democracy, on the interface between democracy and development in Africa, a very robust polemical debate arose in Council for the Development of Economic and Social Research in Africa (CODESRIA) intellectual circles in the 1990s, especially between Thandika Mkandawire and Peter Anyang' Nyong'o (for a review of this debate see Adejumobi 2002). The latter argued that democracy is a sine qua non for development. Citing the experiences of Mauritius and Botswana, both of which achieved some relative economic progress under supposed democratic regimes, Anyang' Nyong'o tasks African scholars and policymakers to take liberal democracy very seriously, as it constitutes the fundamental basis for promoting development. Contrarily, Mkandawire contends that democracy is a worthwhile social value on its own, which all countries must aspire towards, given the freedom and opportunities that it confers; it should not be conceptually merged with development. Democracy may or may not produce development, and the experience of the Asian Tigers, which were essentially authoritarian regimes with unprecedented record of economic transformation, indicates that development is possible without a full democracy. While democracy is good, it must link concretely to the lives of the citizenry.

The progress recorded in the democratic politics in Africa in the recent times is not without its challenges and constraints. Relish and legacy of authoritarian practices loom large in many countries. Executive dominance, though in decline, remains ubiquitous as the use of discretionary power threatens the growth of democratic dispensations. Limited institutional growth and restraint also poses a challenge to political accountability. Parliaments, judiciary, and opposition political parties—three important democratic institutions—remain suborned in many countries, with little capacity, resources, and autonomous space. Institutions of horizontal accountability, like the anti-corruption and human rights bodies, or the audit departments, do not have the vitality or the capacity to affect effective controls. Political impunity is still rampant.

Politics is still perceived as a 'do or die' affair, in which politicians and political parties stake virtually everything for the accumulation and retention of power. This makes elections suffer from a discounted value in promoting meaningful change in governance. Often the winner-takes-all syndrome prevails. Negotiation of political power is associated with access to public resources. However, the rise and flourishing of civil society portends a good omen for democratic politics in Africa. The possibility of accountability from below is increasing by the day, with the demands of the citizens to rights and opportunities. Civil society claims and agitations, if consistent and sustained, may begin to reshape not only the character of politics but also the nature and the essence of the state.

Negotiating External Influence

Often African states are more attentive to the criticism they receive from international media or external public opinion than the criticism they receive from their own constituents. To understand how African states mediate multiple levels of political obligations to their own national agendas, to their regional/continental obligations, and the global community at large, especially where there are obvious, and sometimes not so obvious, conflicts of interest, I will delve into the source of international law that defines such obligations.

Transformations in the domains of war, war crimes, human rights, democratic participation as well as the environment have substantially shifted the classical regime of sovereignty towards a more eroded interpretation of sovereignty.

Classic regime of sovereignty refers to a state-centric conception of sovereignty, where international law is questioned as a law and any legal obligations outside the national realm is considered entirely optional. Tenants of this view contend that most international 'law' that exists today is a compilation of international conventions and treaty agreements, mutually convenient to the signatory nations or imposed upon them by more powerful nations (Pfaff 2000). This classical conception of sovereignty apprehends international law as being horizontal and voluntary and domestic law as being hierarchical and compulsory.

On the other hand, the new mainstreamed views on sovereignty entrench powers and constraints along with rights and duties in international law that—albeit having been ultimately formulated by states—go beyond the traditional conception of the proper scope and boundaries of states, and can come into conflict, and sometimes contradiction, with the national laws. In this perspective, international law is to be regarded as a law, not because of some higher moral code or by sovereign command but because states freely consented to abide by it. In the absence of supranational authority, it goes without saying that agreements and norms obtained from consent rather than from ultimate authority can be withdrawn, should the agreed-upon norm no longer fit the national interest. As a matter of realpolitik, the classic perception of sovereignty supersedes the liberal one when strategic interests and national pride are at stake. The extent to which states exercise their sovereignty is contingent upon their overall influence at the global scale.

Even in the areas of human rights, where tremendous progress has been made in enforcing the rule of law, the resurgence of the state-centric conception of sovereignty is very present. For instance, some African states have been selective in collaboration with the International Criminal Court (ICC) or international bodies on presumed war crimes, crimes against humanity, and ethnic cleansing. The AU has also voiced the protection of the dignity, sovereignty, and integrity of the continent when prosecutions pose a real threat to peace and stability.

International environmental treaties, regimes, and organisations have placed in question elements of state sovereignty, but have not yet locked the drive for national self-determination and its related 'reasons of state' into a transparent, effective, and accountable global framework (Held 2003). Here, again, national interest determines the extent to which states ratify and abide by international obligations, as illustrated in the case of climate change or trade negotiations. Commitments from ill-negotiated agreements result—often—in reversals, especially when explicit sanctions are not defined. In the absence of a supranational enforcement mechanism, it goes without saying that agreements and norms obtained from consent, rather than from ultimate authority, can be withdrawn or violated. Beyond one country's interests, compliance with international obligations is contingent upon a successful dynamic, wherein countries assume both regional and global obligations, while internalising them into the domestic law. Such process leads to a reconstruction of national interests and, eventually, national identities (Koh 1997).

On the quality and content of the democratic process in Africa, while progress is limited and uneven (ECA 2011, 2013), there is some consensus in terms of the understanding that the nature of politics is changing in Africa. Citizens' political participation is on the increase, there is better observance of the rule of law, political freedom is widening, conflicts have largely receded, and, with increasing political stability and predictable political environment, steady economic growth has also been registered. Executive arrogation of power, which, hitherto, was a dominant culture of public life, is being redefined as other institutions of democracy, namely the parliament, the judiciary, media, and civil society, which are gradually checking power excesses. Let us agree that Africa's democracy remains fragile and tenuous and that the possibility of many reversals lurks in the background. The Ibrahim Index on African Governance (IIAG 2015), says it all: Africa's governance performance improved for a decade until 2015 but is now stalling, and will continue to stall until all the challenges and issues outlined above are addressed head-on.

Africa remains a continent in transition: a continent in which both domestic and external forces are exerting impacts upon the nature of its politics and economy. Assessing the current status of African politics, in its inherent complexity and variety, therefore, requires social analytical approaches and methodological tools that consider a cognisance of history, social structure, differences based on the social identities versus individual identities, geographical and cultural context, political agency, to frame the institutional framework of political action and policy. Change happens in specific contexts, not in clean vacuum.

How could I have imagined that a telephone would teach me so much? My latest-generation smartphone does not inspire me like the bulky instrument I discovered when I was ten, but it is a giant reminder that politics will never be the same. In Africa, or anywhere else, because now with national and global integration on grounds of economy and politics, astray strands are coming closer than before, just as the smartphone revolution has been wielding the presence of one large family, despite the inherent differences in the social framework.

References

Adejumobi, S. (2002). Between Democracy and Development: What Are the Missing Links? In B. Abdalla & S. Adejumobi (Eds.), *Breaking Barriers, Creating New Hopes: Democracy, Civil Society and Good Governance in Africa* (pp. 153–172). Trenton: Africa World Press.

Ake, C. (1981). *A Political Economy of Africa*. New York: Longman.

Ake, C. (2000). *The Feasibility of Democracy in Africa*. Dakar: CODESRIA.

Amin, S. (1976). *Unequal Development: An Essay on the Social Formations of Peripheral Capitalism*. New York: Monthly Review Press.

Amin, S. (1978). *Accumulation on a World Scale*. New York: Monthly Review Press.

Amin, S. (1990). *Delinking: Towards a Polycentric World*. London: Zed Books.

Anyang' Nyong'o, P. (Ed.). (1987). *Popular Struggles for Democracy in Africa*. Tokyo: United Nations University.

Anyang' Nyong'o, P. (1989). *African Politics and the Crisis of Development*. Trenton, NJ: Africa World Press.

Bayart, J. F. (1993). *The State in Africa: The Politics of the Belly*. London: Longman.

Boafo-Arthur, K. (Ed.). (2007). *Ghana: One Decade of the Liberal State*. Dakar, London: CODESRIA and Zed Books.

Chabal, P., & Daloz, J.-P. (1999). *Africa Works: Disorder as Political Instrument*. Oxford, Bloomington: James Currey and Indiana University Press.

Chazan, N., Lewis, P., Mortimer, R. A., Rothchild, D., & Stedman, S. J. (1999). *Politics and Society in Contemporary Africa*. Boulder, CO: Lynne Rienner Publishers.

Chole, E., & Ibrahim, J. (Eds.). (1995). *Democratization Processes in Africa: Problems and Prospects*. Dakar: CODESRIA.

ECA. (2011). *Economic Report on Africa: Governing Development in Africa. The Role of the State in Economic Transformation*. Addis Ababa: ECA.

ECA. (2013). *Millennium Development Goals Report 2013: Assessing Progress in Africa Towards the Millennium Development Goals Food Security in Africa – Issues, Challenges and Lessons.* Addis Ababa: ECA.

Ekeh, P. (1975). Colonialism and the Two Publics: A Theoretical Statement. *Comparative Study in Society and History, 17*(1), 91–112.

Held, D. (2003). The Changing Structure of International Law: Sovereignty Transformed? In D. Held & A. McGrew (Eds.), *The Global Transformations Reader: An Introduction to the Globalization Debate.* Cambridge: Polity.

IIAG. (2015). *Ibrahim Index of African Governance 2015.* London: Mo Ibrahim Foundation.

Koh, H. H. (1997). *Why Do Nations Obey International Law?* Faculty Scholarship Series, Paper 2101. Retrieved April 29, 2015, from http://digitalcommons.law.yale.edu/fss_papers/2101.

Lumumba-Kasongo, T. (Ed.). (2005). *Liberal Democracy and Its Critics in Africa.* Dakar: CODESRIA.

Mafeje, A. (1971). The Ideology of Tribalism. *The Journal of Modern African Studies, 9*(2), 253–261.

Mafeje, A. (1991). *The Theory and Ethnography of African Social Formations: The Case of Interlacustrine Kingdoms.* Dakar: CODESRIA.

Mamdani, M. (1996). *Citizen and Subject: Contemporary Africa and the Legacy of Late Colonialism.* Princeton, NJ: Princeton University Press.

Mamdani, M. (Ed.). (2005). *African Studies in Social Movements and Democracy.* Dakar: CODESRIA.

Mamdani, M., Mkandawire, T., & Wamba dia Wamba, E. (1988). *Social Movements, Social Transformation and the Struggle for Democracy in Africa.* Dakar: CODESRIA.

Mkandawire, T. (2013). *Neo-patrimonialism and the Political Economy of Economic Performance in Africa.* Working Paper 1, Stockholm: Institute for Future Studies.

Murunga, G., & Nasongo, S. (Eds.). (2007). *Kenya: The Struggle for Democracy.* Dakar, London: CODESRIA and Zed Books.

Nabudere, D. (1978). *The Political Economy of Imperialism.* London: Zed Books.

Nnoli, O. (1980). *Ethnic Politics in Nigeria.* Enugu: Fourth Dimension Publishers.

Nnoli, O. (Ed.). (1989). *Ethnic Conflict in Africa.* Dakar: CODESRIA.

Nzongola-Ntalaja, G. (1987). *Revolution and Counter-Revolution in Africa.* London: Zed Books.

Nzongola-Ntalaja, G., & Lee, M. (Eds.). (1997). *The State and Democracy in Africa.* Harare: AAPS.

Olukoshi, A. (Ed.). (1998). *The Politics of Opposition in Contemporary Africa.* Uppsala: Nordic Africa Institute.

Onimode, B. (1988). *The Political Economy of the African Crisis.* London: Zed Books and the Institute of African Alternatives.

Osaghae, E. (2001). Federalism and the Ethnic Question in Africa. In J. M. Mbaku, A. Pita Ogaba, & M. Kimenyi (Eds.), *Ethnicity and Governance in the Third World* (pp. 33–57). Aldershot: Ashgate.

Osaghae, E. (2003). *Colonialism and Civil Society in Africa: The Perspectives of Ekeh's Two Publics.* Paper Delivered at the Symposium on Canonical Works and Continuing Innovation in African Arts and Humanities, Accra, Ghana.

Otite, O. (1990). *Ethnic Pluralism and Ethnicity in Nigeria.* Ibadan: Shaneson Limited.

Pfaff, W. (2000). Judging War Crimes. *Survival, 42*(1), 46–58.

Rodney, W. (1972). *How Europe Underdeveloped Africa.* London: Bogle-L'Ouverture Publications.

Van de Walle, N. (2007). *Neopatrimonialism: Democracy and Clientelism in Africa Today.* Working Paper 3–07, Mario Einaudi Center for International Studies, Cornell University.

CHAPTER 3

Respecting Diversity

Pan-Africanism brought in its wake the much-celebrated political liberation that saw Africa overcome domination and oppression, by ending colonialism and Apartheid in the continent. But it is time to admit that, perhaps, those achievements were celebrated a little too quickly. The reality is that, despite decades of independence, the daily realities confronting Africa have not done much to alleviate the problems of poverty, widening inequalities, unemployment, hunger, and general human insecurity.

There are no reasons to ignore the good. Some achievements are startling. Africa tripled its GDP in the last 20 years, achieved amazing gains in the sectors of health and education, improved governance, created the second-most attractive region for investment, and affected a reduction of poverty, despite a demographic explosion that has created the fastest-growing urbanisation drive observed in human history.

It is natural, therefore, that the continent has become more ambitious, bolder, and capable of articulating a long-term vision. The point remains, nevertheless: Is Africa going to construct this bright future with or without a new sense of humanism and fraternity? There resides whatever value we can attribute to the pan-African project.

The philosophical underpinnings of humanism refer to

> humankind's desire and increased ability to rely on its own resources, to master the forces of nature and turn it to its own advantage; and its association with the moral sphere of human existence, in answer to the perennial question of how we should best live. (Pietersen 2005: 45)

C. Lopes, *Africa in Transformation*,
https://doi.org/10.1007/978-3-030-01291-5_3

The twentieth century has reshaped the meaning of humanism to encompass the broad and rising social movement that promotes humanistic values and counters the impersonal and destructive forces of humankind's inhumanity against itself (Pietersen 2005; Edeh 2015). Humanism is opposed to war, tyranny, unjust and oppressive political systems, hierarchy, autocracy, inhumane treatment of people, and any policy rule or institutions that are detrimental to human dignity, integrity, and overall wellbeing. Humanists posit the existence of a community that binds every individual to all others.

The concept of an African humanism cannot be any different. In South Africa, the idea of humanism is referred to as Ubuntu. It represents a philosophy centred on collective will, the principle that humans cannot live in isolation, and do not even exist without the other. Desmond Tutu, who graced the previous Gerwel lecture, sees Ubuntu as the 'essence of being human' (Tutu 1999).

THE ENDURING APPEAL OF PAN-AFRICANISM

How does humanism coexist with the pan-African ideal? Historical examination of pan-Africanism can lead us to three key periods that have shaped the understanding of what this concept entails.

The first wave started outside of the continent, where after the abolition of slavery, Africans in the diaspora were looking for an identity. Questions, such as, 'Who are we?', 'Where did we come from?', and, most importantly, 'How do we find our roots?' were posited. This became the impetus for the pan-African Congresses, the Harlem Renaissance of culture and arts, or the 'Blackness' movement, with several newspapers focussing on identity consciousness, such as Présence Africaine, launched in Paris by Alioune Diop, Negro World by Marcus Garvey, or the Crisis by William DuBois.

This period became known for the firming up of black consciousness, the identity of one's blackness, and the creation of several concepts around the issue of the identity of the blacks. In this mix, African students also found a place, who, on scholarship to study in the countries of their colonial masters, easily identified themselves with the same causes. These African students would mostly end up playing a key role in transporting these new-born ideas to the continent.

The institutions of this time were faced with limited mobilisation, poor representation, and inadequate resources. These institutions were based on passion, a strong belief in the cause of total emancipation, and courage. They made the dream of independence seem attainable, and they influenced the ideology of the liberation movements that fought for the realisation of such an objective.

The second wave of pan-Africanism occurred during the period of euphoria that came with the independences of the 1960s and their aftermath. The leaders of the pan-African movement metamorphosed into political leaders of the newly independent African states, or were advisers to the same. We know that DuBois, for example, relocated to Ghana as a special guest of President Kwame Nkrumah and director of Encyclopaedia Africana, a project he could not finish before his death. Others, such as George Padmore and Ras Makonnen, held positions of power in the newly independent states.

The move from consciousness to affirmation was driven by African intellectuals, who assumed leadership positions in the continent. The Organisation of African Unity (OAU), established on 25 May 1963, in Addis Ababa, with 32 signatories, symbolises the appeal of the pan-African ideal. Though the creation of this body was originally fraught with conflict, it never flinched its focus on the total liberation of the continent.

The third and most recent wave is epitomised by the transformation of the OAU into the AU. What is significantly different between the two is a new focus on development and a shift, one that is more recently articulated, towards transformation.

Pan-Africanism, as an intellectual concept, is, at best, misunderstood, and, at worse, confusing. Several competing but similar meanings were given to the concept of pan-Africanism throughout its history since conception. Nowadays, most see pan-Africanism as encompassing the processes that make a constellation of African states an economically viable and integrated entity.

It is remarkable how the concept remains alive when it is so ill-defined. It is attractive to academics, policymakers, and activists alike, so much so that as the AU celebrated 50 years of African institutional history, in 2013, the theme chosen was, obviously, 'pan-Africanism and the African Renaissance'. To understand this continuous attraction, maybe, it would help to take a detour and revisit the concept of orientalism.

In his 1978 ground-breaking book, *Orientalism*, Palestinian author Edward Said postulated that the term 'orientalism' as a classification was a fabrication of the Western intellectuals in their quest to define the myriad of groups, religions, and nations in the Middle East. This classification sets out to mark the people of the Middle East in a stereotypical way. This classification, nevertheless, took hold to the point wherein the classified started using and owning it, given their own need for alterity.

In an ironic twist, the term 'pan-Africanism' was created by blacks and Africans in the diaspora as a means of self-classification as well as alterity. It was an indirect response to Hegel, the German philosopher, and his depiction of Africans as people without history. In a way, orientalism and pan-Africanism correspond to similar needs, and they provoked similar identity calls.

To this day, the process of correcting the wrong and harmful prejudices against Africans is not over, and may well be responsible for the appeal of the pan-African ideology. No matter how it is defined, until Africans are persuaded that their negative stereotyping is over, pan-Africanism is likely to be a great mutant to build self-confidence.

Yet, Africa's narrative is changing. There is no doubt that the continent's agency is more visible and recognised. However, who is currently writing the Africa story? To a considerable extent, it continues to be driven externally. It is also, often, not a consensual story, as it emanates from either business eagerness or stereotypical perceptions of Afro-stigmatism that continue to persist, despite the economic strides made. The views about Africa 'new times' being about others' opportunities are increasingly patronising and out of touch, posing a deterrent to real interest for transformation and, therefore irritating Africans to the core. There is need for the right balance between realistic descriptions and formulations of 'Africanism' that should include distinct identity cleavages.

NEGATIVE PERCEPTIONS

American 'bestseller' writer Paul Theroux's recent offering about Africa, *The Last Train to Zona Verde: Overland from Cape Town to Angola*, is an attempt to assess just what the twenty-first century has done to Africa in terms of misrepresenting the 'African' story. The book is an example of Afro-pessimism at its best, laced with poor 'stereotypical' descriptions and contradictions, in a bid to live an African fantasy.

For example, by describing a group of Kung people of northeast Namibia, Theroux indulges in describing them as 'mostly naked men and women … an infant with a head like a fuzzy fruit bobbing in one woman's sling, men in leather clouts clutching spears and bows' (Theroux 2013: 5). Someone familiar with the place knows that these are staged scenes to show folkloric Africa. His description is so daunting, archaic, and clichéd, that the readers may think they are reading the works of an early twentieth-century author, maybe Joseph Conrad, or indeed some speech from King Leopold I of Belgium, the then personal owner of the Congo. Perhaps, the pathetic undertones are not surprising, given that the author's own mortality is a recurring theme.

Paul Theroux concludes:

> I had nothing to complain about—but the misery of Africa, the awful, poi-soned, populous Africa; the Africa of cheated, despised, unaccommodated people, of seemingly unfixable blight: so hideous, really, it is unrecognisable as African at all. But it is of course—the new Africa. (Theroux 2013: 34)

The Last Train to Zona Verde is, no doubt, an uncompromising, unsettling work. But it is a bestseller, even in *Exclusive* and other bookstores in South Africa, which goes on to show how misrepresentation is finding consumption at home and overseas.

Another highly regarded and bestselling account of contemporary Africa is the *New York Times* Nairobi correspondent Jeffrey Gettleman's book *Love, Africa: A Memoir of Romance, War and Survival* (2017). With all the aura that the *Times* confers it could have been expected to have a denser assessment of the problems facing the continent. Gettleman's is not as ridiculed as Theroux's but still associates itself to the exceptionalism, adventure-image of Africa. His anedocte about how editors prepared him for the assignment with advice for him to be cautions and 'not get too ooga-booga out there' is preposterous. While another senior colleague gives the opposite advice—'Don't forget the ooga-booga. It's what makes Africa Africa'—which captures the essence of what he conveys. An attempt to be fair, but with glasses that are marked.

Bad stories about Africa by outsiders are dismissed as being normal. What should count is the narrative constructed by the Africans. I defend this viewpoint. But I also maintain that it should not be about hiding facts, particularly the bad examples we set for ourselves.

The xenophobic episodes that occurred in South Africa caught the public opinion across the continent, fracturing the ideal of pan-Africanism. Many were quick to remind South Africans about the sacrifices of the continent for their liberation from Apartheid, considering such utter dismissal of other Africans' dignity. It was unacceptable that the pan-African ideal, many said, could be trashed in such a way. Few remembered, however, that similar expulsions or beatings of fellow Africans occurred with declared government support in at least 15 other African countries before. Arguably, the largest mass expulsion took place in Nigeria in 1983 and 1985, when three million West Africans were beaten all the way to the borders. The expulsion of Africans by fellow Africans is not just a South African issue. It is a recurrent African problem. Fellow Africans have been mass-expelled from Cameroon, Chad, Equatorial Guinea, Ghana, Kenya, Nigeria, Senegal, Sierra Leone, Uganda, the Democratic Republic of Congo, Zambia, Gabon, and, more recently, from Libya and Algeria.

Africans have been moving around quite a bit. In pre-colonial times, it was often driven by the need to find land for settlement and fertile expanses for farming. Colonial regimes altered those motivations to reflect migratory patterns that reflected political and economic structures imposed by the colonial regimes. The impact of this remains till date.

Thus, one can argue that the more recent events reinforce the daily struggles that Africans are confronted with, due to the absence of the economic and political changes that should have followed the liberation struggles or political transitions. The failure of Africa to provide a reality that complements the aspirations of its citizens reinforces Amílcar Cabral's premonition, that the reality for which people exist, indeed the reason why people are willing to fight, is to obtain practical things, like peace and better living conditions (Lopes 2010).

The Westphalian conceptualisation of the African state is another pertinent point to consider when speaking out the shifting identity dynamics, which is the focus of this chapter; if we assess the trajectory of the contemporary African state, we recognise more Westphalian than pan-African traits.

The Westphalian state is premised upon the notion of sovereignty and the exclusion of all external powers in the domestic affairs of the state. At the genesis of the Westphalian state are the treaties celebrated in that city in 1648. They marked the recognition of sovereignty, based on principles quite different from the previous forms of political legitimacy. Indeed, this premise assumed the presence of a functioning government. There is no need to revisit the full spectrum of developments that ensued to realise that the principle of sovereignty was controversial, provoked many wars, including two across the globe, but ended up imposing itself in the form of what we now call international community, with its myriad international organisations.

The emergence of current global governance mechanisms, as well as the body of existing international law, and, indeed, regional institutions have all their foundations in the Westphalian state model.

All entities that, as latecomers, were integrated into the established order imposed as the aftermath of two World Wars found the landscape of international relations already defined. All they wanted was to be part of it and to claim their fair share through the recognition of their sovereignty. This was the case with post-colonial Africa, who, it has been argued, embraced the Westphalian state in all its totality. This is still the case, but centripetal forces are not helping. The erosion of sovereignty is the new normal with international treaties and agreements calling for transnational and global modes of intervention. Perhaps one of the most remarkable developments of the last two decades has been the proclivity of the 'international community' to intervene in different countries with social and political rights justifications that go way beyond the humanitarian concepts of the 1950s (Rao 2010).

Every conflict in Africa that relates to the definition of territory, or is trying to address the issue of legitimacy or lack of it, by a central authority, is, in fact, revisiting the chequered history of the sovereignty principle. A current case in point would be the Burundian government challenging interference from others on what it considers as its internal affairs; or religiously motivated or justified movements, fighting for geographical space and independence from central authority in Nigeria, Mali, or Libya.

Responses from African institutions have been short term in nature, with scarce analysis of the deep-rooted causes motivating the conflicts. This is partly explained by the desire for Africa to be perceived as being compliant with the international order, so it can move fast into the catching-up mode that characterises the current state of its international relations.

Being Westphalian explains why expulsions are possible and a common African passport is not, despite the pan-African rhetoric. It is not a South African problem alone; it is the very essence of defining what the true meaning of pan-Africanism is today.

It is against this background that we hear in Africa, as elsewhere, the call for the adoption of a cosmopolitan view (Sen 2007; Appiah 2015), when addressing the shifting identity dynamics. Cosmopolitism is a strengthened Western formulation of secularism. The origin of the word alone—from the Greek *cosmos* and *polis*, signifying the wide and the particular forms of interaction and knowledge—tells us how sophisticated a concept it is. Cosmopolitism presupposes a desire to construct alliances and amplify community relationships by embracing diversity and expansion on a global scale. It is an ambiguous attempt to reconcile universal values with the unique realities that subjects construct in specific historical and cultural contexts (Ribeiro 2003).

The ambiguity extends to the way most translate secularism in an environment where international institutions format rules around individual rights, lessening the community and the larger group interpretation of rights (Ribeiro 2003). Without us necessarily linking it with the reality of conflicts or, to our disappointment, with a hypothetical diminishing political agency of Africans at the world stage, the truth is that cosmopolitism is a source of tension, when employing this as a tool of identity-formation.

Globalisation is based on interpretations of the cosmopolitism foundations (Appiah 2015). According to Pryker (2009), we are dealing with the tension between the general and the particular, the former being expressed through globalisation and the latter through resurgent nationalism. I would refine this stance by adding religiously motivated contestation to this list as well.

> Try as we might, binaries, oppositions, perceive contradictions, call them what you will, are difficult things to escape from as they organize our thoughts and allow us to think through problems. The real problem with globalization versus national dichotomy is that it can too easily be used by those who are sceptical about globalization. That is because it is easy enough to show that globalization has little significant impact on the resilience of nationalism. (Pryker 2009: 56)

The pan-African ideology, constructed first by the African diaspora, has remained a strong anchor for the continent's common vision. It is a concept that has travelled well, with its ambiguities not disturbing a common ambition and a common reference to the recent past. It has been reinterpreted many times, if not reenergised. However, we all know its limitations when it comes to dealing with the complexity of cosmopolitism.

The shyness that African leaders show along with other fellow Africans, when the theme of migration is brought up, is disturbing, but not surprising. Still, it does not give us the full story. The adjustment required by Africans to integrate the mainstream international relations exercises a pull factor that has proven to be more solid in terms of impact than the desire to defend a joint, common African agency in all that matters.

Current attacks and intolerances call for an African humanism that strikes a balance between pan-Africanism, the Westphalian conception of the African State, and cosmopolitanism, while giving sufficient space to the plurality underlying the African identity, while showcasing how it all informs the broad concept of American humanism while retaining all its distinct textures and nuances. Africa cannot forget its rich cultural heritage and its history of struggle for freedom.

There is a need for a revival that recovers African identities distorted by colonialism, along with addressing the problems of the twenty-first century, such as environmental regeneration, inequality, or new forms of conflict. These challenges demand the construction of a common African future, based on a bold transformative agenda that goes beyond just the economic results. I argue that the myth of African solidarity has to be put aside, if transformation is taken seriously. Frank and honest assessments are to be made about the institutional and political behaviour that has allowed continuous infringements of minority and marginalised groups rights.

Africa's transformation and its contribution to forging a new humanism will be elusive in the absence of shared freedoms, shared prosperity, and a common citizenship within and across borders.

REFERENCES

Appiah, K. A. (2015). *Cosmopolitanism: Ethics in a World of Strangers*. London: Penguin.

Edeh, P. D. (2015). African Humanism in Achebe in Relation to the West. *Open Journal of Philosophy, 5*(3), 205–210.

Gettleman, J. (2017). *Love, Africa: A Memoir of Romance, War and Survival*. London: Harper Collins.

Lopes, C. (Ed.). (2010). *Africa's Contemporary Challenges: The Legacy of Amílcar Cabral*. New York: Routledge.

Pietersen, H. J. (2005). Western Humanism, African Humanism and Work Organizations. *South African Journal of Industrial Psychology, 31*(3), 54–61.

Pryker, S. (2009). *Nationalism in a Global World*. London: Palgrave Macmillan.

Rao, R. (2010). *Third World Protest: Between Home and the World*. New York: Oxford University Press.

Ribeiro, L. G. (2003). *Post-imperialismo: Cultura y Política en el Mundo Contemporáneo*. Barcelona: Editorial Gedisa.

Sen, A. (2007). *Identity and Violence*. New York: WW Norton.

Theroux, P. (2013). *The Last Train to Zona Verde: Overland from Cape Town to Angola*. London: Penguin Books.

Tutu, D. (1999). *No Future Without Forgiveness*. London: Ebury Publishing.

CHAPTER 4

Understanding Policy Space

With the devastating crisis that hit most of the wealthy countries and the failure of the financial systems, we have now entered a new era, characterised by both conjectural and structural changes. It entails a profound transformation that affects the perception and the distribution of power. For almost three decades mainstream policy has been framed on the basis of neo-classic economic theory, modernised by the interpretation given by the Washington Consensus.

The term 'Washington Consensus' comes from a simple set of ten recommendations identified by economist John Williamson in 1989, which are as follows: (1) fiscal discipline; (2) redirecting public expenditure; (3) tax reform; (4) financial liberalisation; (5) adoption of a single, competitive exchange rate; (6) trade liberalisation; (7) elimination of barriers to foreign direct investment (FDI); (8) privatisation of state-owned enterprises; (9) deregulation of market entry and competition; and (10) a securing of property rights. The reference to 'Consensus' meant that this list was premised on the ideas shared at the time by power circles in Washington, including the US Congress and administration, on one hand, and international institutions such as the Washington-based IMF and the World Bank, on the other, supported by a range of think tanks and influential economists.

It is important to note here that the theoretical foundations underlying these policy recommendations were nothing else but neo-classical economics, espousing a firm belief in the market's 'invisible hand', the

© The Author(s) 2019
C. Lopes, *Africa in Transformation*,
https://doi.org/10.1007/978-3-030-01291-5_4

rationality of the economic actors' choices, and a minimalist vision of the states' regulation of economies. The advent of this new paradigm has also marked the retreat of development economics as a distinct field that had been long dominated by the 'Dependency School' and other theories (Naim 1999), often in sharp contrast with neo-classical economics and methodological individualism. It was development economics that had often guided policies experimented with in the developing countries, before the Washington Consensus era. Most independent African governments, for example, sought to promote industrialisation, develop local production and reduce imports, promote employment, raise the standard of living, and break out of the vicious circle of trade patterns epitomised in the Prebisch-Singer hypothesis (unfavourable terms of trade for commodity-exporting and manufacturer-importing countries). The Washington Consensus' recipes, by contrast, were presented as bearing universality, similarly applicable in the context of developed and developing countries, even if they ended up being implemented in a discriminatory and an uneven fashion.

Washington Consensus policies were applied for more than two decades in such diverse contexts as Africa, Latin America, and Asia, along with being implemented in countries in political and economic transition in Eastern Europe and Central Asia. There were usually two major stages of intervention: the first focused on macroeconomic stability and structural adjustment programs, and the second included such objectives as improving institutions, reducing corruption, or dealing with infrastructural inefficiency (Naim 1999). The conditionality exercised by the Bretton Woods institutions and wealthy countries played a crucial role in the indebted countries' decisions to push through macroeconomic stabilisation reforms and structural adjustment programs. The debt crisis that first affected several Latin American countries and then the African and Asian countries in the 1970s and 1980s, further increasing their dependence on external loans, left them with no other option than to follow the prescriptions that enabled them to access financing, and this is where things went wrong.

What Exactly Went Wrong?

Washington Consensus policies have been criticised since the 1990s by a sizeable number of leading economists. Most notably, Joseph Stiglitz, chief economist at the World Bank from 1997 to 2000, criticised the policies prescribed by the IMF in response to the financial crises in Russia and

Asia (Stiglitz 2003, 2007, 2013); Paul Krugman (2008) was in favour of Asian governments imposing controls on capital flows in 1997–1998. The debate generated over the response to the crisis provided a good illustration of the deep divide between leading economists, who either supported or opposed the IMF. The Washington Consensus purists insisted on the importance of stabilising exchange rates in times of crisis through public budget cuts, higher taxes and interest rates, and other recessive measures. Their opponents criticised such policies, arguing that they would lead to a recession (Naim 1999). Stiglitz called attention to the fact that sharp increases in interest rates would contribute towards the deepening of the crisis (Stiglitz 2003, 2013).

It is now commonplace to say that structural adjustment and macro-economic stabilisation programmes had a disastrous impact on social policies and poverty levels in many countries. However, it is important to analyse the negative consequences in order to learn from the previous mistakes Following the first wave of reforms undertaken by debt-affected African and Latin American countries—which included public expenditure cuts, introduction of charges for health and education, and reductions in industrial protection, leading to high unemployment, poverty rise, and unequal income distribution—the United Nations International Children's Emergency Fund (UNICEF) published the report *Adjustment with a Human Face* (1987), which called for 'meso-policies' to be redirected towards protecting social and economic sectors that were essential to the survival of the poor through the introduction of social protection programs.

Speaking of the negative consequences, the period of structural adjustment programmes in the sub-Saharan Africa in the 1980s was characterised by poor economic performance. The GDP rose by less than 1% in Africa between 1979 and 1992, whereas in the East Asia and the Pacific regions, where the state played an active role in promoting industrial and social policies as well as in poverty alleviation, an average growth of 5% between 1986 and 1992 was registered. African investments declined, and the continent's share in the world exports also fell by more than one-half between 1975 and 1990. The share of Africa in agricultural and food exports dropped from 21% to 8.1% of developing countries' exports, and in manufactured goods exports, from 7.8% in 1980 to 1.1% in 1990. Some critics pointed out that liberalisation policies, and such policies as the elimination of subsidies for fertilisers, had a negative impact on agricultural productivity and output. Price reform promoted export crops over traditional food crops. Others argued that export crops contributed to indebtedness, or that adjustment programmes exacerbated unequal land distribution, promising that 'efficient' land markets would replace traditional tenure systems, while encouraging deindustrialisation through 'wholesale privatisation and unfettered markets' (Sahn et al. 1997: 1–6).

One of the major drawbacks of the policies imposed by the IMF and the World Bank was the lack of technical expertise and strategic capability on the part of the implementing countries. A structurally unequal donor-recipient relationship was established, in part due to the weakening of the public sector induced by the drastic reduction of the administrative machine. The fast and uncontrolled liberalisation of small African economies presented additional dangers, such as the high volatility of capital flows, but, as a then South African Finance Minister said in 2003:

> A larger problem for African economies is that their growth potential is directly affected by their ability to export and use export revenue to diversify production. Their ability to do so is constrained by a global trade regime inimical to the full development of African countries' comparative advantage. Limited market access for low-cost textiles, cotton, and agricultural products and competition from heavily subsidized industrial economy exports effectively prevent growth. (Manuel 2003: 18)

The social impact of these reforms was devastating for sub-Saharan Africa. Many economists recognised that the difficulties associated with the promotion of economic stability and liberalisation had a disproportionate impact on the poor, leading to greater poverty and unequal income distribution. International financial institutions (IFIs), particularly the World Bank, displayed great intellectual arrogance in failing to acknowledge for a long time the vastly negative impact of such policies, denying the criticisms levelled at them and limiting their response to launching compensatory programmes (Sahn et al. 1997: 6).

It is, thus, not surprising that macroeconomic stabilisation and structural adjustment policies prompted a wave of popular unrest that contributed to the recrudescence of many civil wars in the 1990s. The 1997 Asian crisis also raised some important questions about the consequences of the deregulation of financial markets and demonstrated the limits of the Washington-based policy thought.

THE STRUCTURAL CONSEQUENCES OF THE WASHINGTON CONSENSUS

The rapid economic growth registered in many regions of the South in the first decade of the twenty-first century, accompanied by expanding trade and investment, offset the worries of the financial markets, which ignored the signs of the impending storm. In 2008, however, the crème de la crème of the economist profession, as well as the governments of rich countries, finally had to face the inconvenient truth about the imperfection of the markets in currency. Massive and uncontrolled financial speculation had produced the worst global economic crisis since the Great Depression, suddenly revealing a number of structural 'diseases' that the Washington Consensus had been hiding under the rug.

The global downturn was a revelation in two major respects. First, the domination of the financial sector over the real economy had led to unpredictability concerning the future of economies and increased vulnerability of populations, simultaneously increasing unequal income distribution and the gap between the rich and poor. Second, it called into question the prevailing economic theories that served as a basis for formulating and prescribing policies, including those formulated by Bretton Woods institutions at the global level, in particular the structural adjustment programs.

After three decades of the implementation of the formulations of the Washington Consensus, we have been witnessing a confluence of crises, including spikes in food and energy prices as well as financial and economic downturn, further aggravated by the impact of global climate change and growing demography. An article that I co-authored with Ignacy Sachs and Ladislau Dowbor stresses upon the striking convergence of critical tendencies, 'the synergy of behaviours that [...] are destroying our fragile spaceship', referring to the interdependence of trends in areas traditionally considered separately, such as demography, climate, industrial and agricultural production and consumption, pollution, to cite a few (Lopes et al. 2010: 1, 3).

There is now absolute awareness of the growing inequalities and the scandalous concentration of income, following the Washington Consensus—with the richest 20% getting more than 80% of the global income (Lopes et al. 2010: 5). The dramatic rise in the share of poor people living in the so-called emerging countries reveals how unequal income distribution is turning out to be, even in rapidly growing economies: 72% of the poor populace worldwide currently live in the middle-income countries, whereas two decades ago, 93% lived in the low-income countries. In the current structure of power, economic growth, even when generated by technological innovation, benefits the financial intermediaries that pursue short-term maximisation of profits rather than the engineers of the process (Lopes et al. 2010: 5).

Productive inclusion, as reflected in the formal sector, is the exception rather than the rule. Production and consumption patterns reveal an abnormal deformation of priorities, where military budgets and luxury consumer goods are given precedence over access to basic services, education, and health:

> The planet produces almost a kilo of grain per day per inhabitant and we have more than one billion people going hungry. The ten million children who die of hunger, no access to clean water and other absurd causes constitutes an unbearable scandal. But from the private investment point of view, solving essential problems generates no profits, and the orientation of our production capacity is radically deformed. (Lopes et al. 2010: 7)

These systemic failures are principally due to a skewed configuration of the production processes, false structures of incentives, and an economic framework that externalises social and environmental costs, relying exclusively on the 'rational choice' of actors and the 'natural' balance of the market—to say nothing of the way the global economy is currently run.

The power imbalance within the global structures of financial and economic governance, namely the IMF and the World Bank, is evident at the following three levels:

- First, at the level of the prevailing ideology, entirely dominated by monetarist thought, imposed on the countries of the South and transition economies for more than 20 years, despite blatant failures and disastrous social impact;
- Second, at the level of the power structure established by voting shares within the IMF and the World Bank, which still does not reflect the size of economies, not to mention the inadequate representation of the interests of the poorest;
- Third, at the level of the strong belief that wealthy countries would never be affected by crises, something that justified discriminatory practices in terms of surveillance before 2008 (IEO 2011), and the application of double standards during the crisis. Thus, the financial crisis that resulted from a spiralling deregulation did not come as a complete surprise.

Concerning the last point, we need only compare the IMF response to the European debt crisis with the policies it implemented in the 1980s and 1990s to attain picture of those double standards. Although there has been a laudable change of attitude, favouring the social dimension instead of the creditors' interests, the fact is that these policies are only being promoted now, in Europe, hypocritically erasing the past.

Where Are We Heading?

The ostensible belief in recipes that do not work and yet continue to be used is somewhat of a paradox. When theoretical tools designed to help comprehend reality are used without any consideration of their limitations, or when findings are selectively adjusted to endorse one single view premised on wishful thinking, then science turns into ideology. Globalisation, as it emerged and was perceived, over the last decade of the twentieth century, prompted a wave of opposition. The most radical and vocal opponents of the Washington Consensus accused Bretton Woods institutions and the wealthy countries of spreading a new ideology—that of neo-liberalism. Leading economists got blinded by the myth of perfect markets, either by choice or by circumstance. As Paul Krugman sarcastically put it, 'the economics profession went astray because economists, as a group, mistook beauty, clad in impressive-looking mathematics, for truth' (Krugman 2009: MM36).

The neo-classical notion of market efficiency—challenged way back by John Maynard Keynes, who called for active government intervention in the marketplace by printing more money and increasing public spending to boost demand during the Great Depression—returned to currency in the last decade. The truth is that the blind belief in markets has enjoyed great popularity, until it was stopped by the current populist wave.

Led by Milton Friedman, monetarism invaded economic thought in the 1970s, seeking to reconcile macroeconomics with neo-classical microeconomic postulates, to bring the idea of market efficiency back to the centre stage. Monetarists admitted only limited forms of government intervention, linked to a very modest regulation of money supply. Famously, Milton Friedman called for the dissolution of the IMF, since it interfered with the workings of the free market. Many macroeconomists completely rejected the Keynesian theory regarding expansive stimulus during economic crises, and others returned to the view forwarded by Schumpeter and other apologists for the Great Depression, viewing 'recessions as a good thing, part of the economy's adjustment to change' (Krugman 2009: 36MM).

This debate had a strong influence on the IMF postulates. Without adopting monetarism wholesale, the major concepts of the Washington Consensus provided responses to the IMF's concerns with minimising regulation and letting markets do their work. It was this approach that led the IMF to believe that its main job was to liberalise the market in the countries of the South, and, later, in the so-called transition economies, since these represented the major obstacles to the implementation of an open economy.

The report produced by the IMF's Independent Evaluation Office (IEO) on the failure of the IMF's surveillance role, vehemently criticised its performance on one of its main functions—to warn member countries of the risks building up in the world economy as well as in their national contexts. Among the major impediments identified by the Evaluation Office were 'a high degree of groupthink, intellectual capture, a general mind-set that a major financial crisis in large advanced economies was unlikely, and inadequate analytical approaches' (IEO 2011: 17).

A careful reading of the report's findings reveals additional inconvenient truths. First, intellectual narrow-mindedness creates situations where the line between what we see and what we want to see is too easy to cross. Another important reason for the IMF's failure to report accurately and produce an honest analysis was the influence the largest shareholders exerted on surveillance and policies (IEO 2011: 20).

The IEO drew an unflattering picture of the IMF staff, pointing to 'cognitive biases', including a homogeneous mind-set (groupthink) and an 'insular culture' that rarely referred to external research; the belief that economists in advanced countries were better aware of what was happening in their own countries, overlooking the importance of financial issues and the analysis of macroeconomic linkages; overreliance on models and similar tools, such as macromodelling, which practically did not include the analysis of the financial sophistication of current global transactions and asset markets; overreliance on simplistic and first-round examination techniques, such as stress-testing, to determine the soundness of banking systems; and, worst still, misinterpretation or dismissal of certain data for the sake of theoretical coherence (IEO 2011: 17–19).

Intellectual honesty was further injured by the lack of reference to the limitations of data or to the existence of different analyses. The IMF epitomised the major drawbacks of modern knowledge production and applied research, characterised by sectoral approaches and lack of holistic analysis.

More specifically, it opted for economic theories, along with quantitative and data selection methods that sustained the coherence of its neo-classical assumptions. Dissenting views were silenced, given the power chain reaction between the largest shareholder countries and senior management. The authors of the evaluation report also noted the complaints about lack of even-handedness in the treatment of different countries (IEO 2011: 20). To put it in a nutshell, the main institution in charge of macroeconomic policy recommendations produced an analysis that was heavily influenced by its most powerful members, and the same promoted conformity, self-censorship, data selectivity, and one set of analytical approaches implemented in a discriminatory manner.

It is essential to engage in an honest academic dialogue and to promote intelligent systems of governance that are open to a plurality of approaches and lead to fruitful synergies between the different contributions. Regrettably, however, there are too many cases of bias involved in the collection and interpretation of statistical data. There is a growing awareness of the multifaceted and diverse nature of our world, and of the interconnection between the various challenges that we face. This opens new perspectives on how we can see and interpret the world around us, helping us to think outside the box.

Besides GDP, the Human Development Index (HDI), the Gini coefficient, and the Happiness Index represented important assessments breakthroughs. The number of economic, social, and statistical indicators that can help us understand the importance of demography is growing at a fast pace. For instance, the way in which we currently measure international trade has evolved considerably, although it is not yet catching with the complexity of global value chains (Lamy 2011).

Bearing this in mind, Robert Zoellick, the President of the World Bank between 2007 and 2012, sent an important signal, when he initiated the liberalisation of the Bank's information policy, granting public access to about 7000 data sets that were previously available only to subscribers, mostly governments and researchers. During the first month alone, 4.5 million individual visitors accessed the site. Since these data are used to define social and economic policies, their importance as a bargaining tool is fundamental. The data and methodology underlying the analysis and political recommendations of the World Bank are, thus, open to public scrutiny. Robert Zoellick described his decision as a 'democratization of development economics' (Strom 2011). But true democratisation is more than just making data sets available. Statistical quality, in so far as Africa is concerned, is a debate on its own. Most data sets regarding African economies are outdated methodologically or in terms of real data collection, provoking heavy reliance on projections of questionable quality.

The choice of Justin Lin for the World Bank Chief Economist position (between 2008 and 2012) was in itself a major surprise—a Taiwanese military defector to continental China who turned into an economist with strong advocacy for what he defines as new structural economics. Lin is a strong advocate of his country development model (Lin 2012; Monga and Lin 2015). Nothing could be further from the Washington Consensus proposals.

The IMF also surprised the world when it published, in June 2016, an article in its main magazine, *Finance & Development*, questioning liberalisation claims, and opening further the policy space debate (Ostri et al. 2016). An IMF working paper response to Piketty, now a famous granular study on inequality, seemed to go in an opposite direction. Piketty's central thesis is that when the rate of return on capital is greater than the rate of economic growth, the result is the concentration of wealth in the long term. In turn, such unequal distribution of wealth causes social and economic upheaval. Piketty offered suggestions on how to address issues such as a system of progressive wealth taxes to help reduce inequality and avoid the clear majority of wealth coming under the possession of a tiny minority (Piketty 2013).

The IMF working paper claimed there was no empirical evidence to sustain Piketty's claims (Goes 2016), and yet, inequality became the trademark of IMF's Managing Director Christine Lagarde. Just before the 2017 spring meetings of the IMF and the World Bank two senior IMF officials published a blog post arguing the need for fiscal policies to address inequality (Gaspar and Garcia-Escribano 2017). It recognises 'there is no one-size-fits-all strategy. Redistribution should reflect a country's specific circumstances, including underlying fiscal pressures, social preferences, and the government's administrative and tax capacity. Also, taxes and transfers cannot be considered in isolation' (Gaspar and Garcia-Escribano 2017). This type of flexibility and humility is a considerable shift from traditional IMF approaches. However, on the ground things have not changed as much, prompting some to claim that there is more hypocrisy from the organisation than real change (Sheil and Stilwell 2017).

SIGNIFICANT CHANGES INFLUENCING AFRICA'S ROLE

The sets of indicators one selects for analysis and the way they are collected, defined, and interpreted matters. The divergence in the 1990s between the Washington-based institutions, on one hand, and United Nations, on the other, regarding the impact of structural adjustment reforms provided a compelling example of different recommendations based on different approaches.

The growing influence of the countries from the South, including African countries, is a factor that is contributing to change on many levels. At present, it is no longer affordable to ignore divergences, since the major players and power relations are rapidly changing the dominant ideas. When Goldman Sachs coined the term BRIC (acronym for Brazil, Russia, India, China) in 2001, many did not take it seriously. The 2008–2009 crisis accelerated the shift in the global balance of power, and the G20 took over the leading role from the G7/8. BRICS, now including South Africa, accounts roughly for a quarter of the world's GDP, 15% of global trade, and slightly above 40% of the total population.

In terms of economic relevance, African countries are still relatively marginal in these new mega shifts. However, the continent's improved performance and its rate of return on investment are amongst the world's highest. A study by Ernst & Young indicated that FDI in Africa grew by 87% in the first decade of this century, and that FDI flows continued even during the crisis, and may have even accelerated in 2012 (Ernst & Young 2011: 7). The most recent update of Africa inward FDI trends by Ernst & Young (2017) shows a recovery in 2016 after a dip in 2015, probably the most difficult year since 2000. During 2016, capital investment rose 31.9%. Average investment per project was US $139 million in 2016, against US $92.5 million in 2015. This surge was the result of quite a few large, capital-intensive projects in the real estate, hospitality and construction (RHC), and transport and logistics sectors. Africa's global FDI capital flows share increased to 11.4%, up from 9.4% in 2015. That made Africa the second fastest-growing destination when measured by FDI capital, after South East Asia (Ernst & Young 2017).

The Boston Consulting Group has arrived at similar readings, based on somewhat different data sets, namely an annual growth in exports by 18% since 2000, like the BRICS, and an annual increase of over 8% in the revenues of the 500 largest African companies since 1998. This report (produced before the Arab revolutions) points to the emergence of the so-called African Lions (analogous to the 'Asian Tigers'), which include Algeria, Botswana, Egypt, Libya, Mauritius, Morocco, South Africa, and Tunisia (with a collective GDP per capita of US $10,000, exceeding that of BRICS), soon to be joined by Ghana and Nigeria (BCG 2010: 1–2). A more recent study by McKinsey Global Institute (2016) confirms the trends but warns about the downturn in 2014–2015 and the major impact the so-called Arab Spring and oil prices downfall had on the overall African performance.

The landscape for trade and investment is changing very fast. Outward FDI from developing countries is gathering strength, and with it giving African countries more room for manoeuvre. According to the World Bank (2017) this type of investment has increased 20-fold in the last 20 years, reaching in 2015 one-fifth of total global FDI flows. While the lion's share of these flows originates from the BRICS (Brazil, the Russian Federation, India, China, and South Africa), the fact remains that about 90% of developing countries are now reporting outward FDI. Although comprehensive figures are not available for Africa it is safe to say that the continent has been one of the major destinations for this new investment flows.

The population of Africa has exceeded the one billion indicators. Demographic growth is considered a crucial element in the shift of power from North to East, and then, South, and the fast-growing middle classes, both in emerging countries, such as BRICS, and in Africa, seem to account for a significant part of the global demand. Recent analyses indicate that the lower-middle class in countries of the South represents a huge, fast-growing new market, which will determine various products and services from those that have until now been supplied to the middle classes of wealthy countries.

These recent developments, especially in sub-Saharan Africa, coincide with a period in which the control of IFIs has weakened, opening a space for the reformulation of policies. A good example of such a change is the issuance of a new directive regarding debt sustainability criteria for low-income countries (IMF 2017a), considerably improving the policy space and allowing for contextual issues to be inserted in the assessments. Even the IMF Conditionality manual (2017b) has been updated to reflect lessons from the recent interventions in Europe.

As African countries aggressively pursue industrial policies they are finding a more sympathetic attitude on the part of Bretton Woods institutions. However, the changes do not extend to giving Africa a bigger voice in the governance of these institutions or to radically question the classic framework of the Washington Consensus entirely.

The Impact of the Financial Crisis
on the Washington Consensus

The reconfiguration of economic geography started exerting pressure on the old and inadequate governance structures of the IMF and the World Bank, established after the Second World War. As a result, they began a slow process of reformation that included the redistribution of voting shares. First, the voting share of sub-Saharan Africa rose by 3%, but it continues to represent only 1.4% of the total. After a second round of revisions, China's calculated quota share rose from 6.38% to 7.47%, which placed it ahead of Japan (whose calculated quota declined to 6.99%), but still behind the United States, with its 17.8%. The total share of the European Union (EU) is estimated to fall from 25% in 2000 to 18% in 2015. Similarly, because of the World Bank governance reform, only 3.3% of votes have been transferred from the OECD to the developing countries. China's share rose from 2.77% to 4.42%, thus turning it into the third-largest shareholder after the United States and Japan. However, the United States continues to be the leading player, holding 16.85% of voting shares, while more than one-third of the African countries saw their shares decrease.

The financial downturn signalled the need for more radical transformations within the IMF. In early 2011, the IMF's leadership suggested that SDRs (IMF's Special Drawing Rights, currently composed of the dollar, pound, euro, and yen) could help stabilise the global financial system. For this to happen, their current role as a reserve currency with the Fund's loans denominated in SDRs would need to be substantially expanded to areas such as 'a potential new class of reserve assets: tradable SDR denominated securities issued by the Fund', or 'a unit of account which could be used to price internationally traded assets (e.g., sovereign bonds) or goods (e.g., commodities)'. These suggestions were presented and analysed in a report published by the IMF in January 2011, which argues that 'in order to make a difference in any of these areas, the role played by the SDR would need to be enhanced considerably from its current insignificant level. Very significant practical, political, and legal hurdles would need to be overcome in the process' (IMF 2011: 1). Moreover, it was argued that the inclusion of currencies of the emerging economies in the current SDR basket would help promote such objectives as increasing the supply of safe global assets and 'reducing negative impacts of exchange rate volatility among major currencies' (IMF 2011: 1). Such proposals obviously come close, if anything else, to developing an alternative to the US dollar as the global reserve currency.

The proposals for an alternative reserve currency also reflect the growing influence of emerging economies, whose central banks, particularly in China, are diversifying their foreign currency basket and moving away from the US dollar, which devalued significantly against stronger currencies in the first half of 2011. It should be noted, however, that emerging countries have a high percentage of their reserves in the US treasury bonds, and thus, they want a stronger dollar (Addison 2011).

The major world creditors are now countries of the South, many of which achieved success through policies that challenged the orthodoxy of the Washington Consensus. The IMF's Chief Economist from that time (2008–2015), Olivier Blanchard, recognised that 'in the age-old discussion of the relative roles of markets and the state, the pendulum has swung—at least a bit—toward the state', and that 'distortions within finance are macro-relevant' (Blanchard 2011). This implies a humble stance, but not necessarily a fundamental change.

Indeed, the IMF stance during the European debt crisis was, at times, surprising for those used to the old style of the Washington Consensus. In Ireland, the IMF first appeared as defending the interests of the Irish taxpayers in the face of the European Central Bank and Ireland's creditors, by putting forward a plan to reduce '€30 billion of unguaranteed bonds by two-thirds on average' (Whitney 2011). It later changed to a more traditional role as the Euro area crisis deepened and creditors began to exert pressure. In any case, the macroeconomic policies promoted by some Southeast Asian countries as well as Latin America's fiscal conservatism, coupled with aggressive social policies (through income transfer programs), have long placed the Washington Consensus on the defensive (Stiglitz 2007, 2013; Rodrik 2011; Rajan 2010).

When in 1998 IMF Director General Michel Camdessus, supported by Alan Greenspan and Lawrence Summers, blamed the Asian financial crisis on poor governance and preconised draconian measures to address them, Keynesian-type counter-cyclical were defiantly advocated by Stiglitz (2007, 2013) and Krugman (2008). In the tug of war the calls for a reform of the international financial system got lost. The lowering of interest rates by the US Federal Reserve Bank was the most important contributor to appease the crisis, although it also made the reforms less pressing.

The Post-Washington Consensus Era: New Hope for Economists?

While neo-classical theories are undergoing scrutiny, economists need to remember how Keynes challenged the perfection of markets, particularly financial markets, making the case for regulation. The return of the state onto the scene to correct market failures is inevitable. Ha-Joon Chang kept reminding that industrial policy was for quite some time conspicuous by its absence, despite the successes of the export-oriented industrial policy experience of South Korea, and others in Asia: 'Sustainable export success over an extended period, for which the country is justly famous, requires protection and nurturing of "infant industries" through selective industrial policy, rather than free trade and deregulation'. In contrast to the 'one-size-fits-all' approach promoted by the Washington-based institutions, Koreans spoke of a 'dynamic iPhone model' or 'a set of development apps for every occasion, drawn from successful approaches in different countries' (Chang 2010: 27).

Dani Rodrik (2011) points to a major intellectual change within the development profession that certainly includes growth strategies but also health, education, and other social policies. He contrasts a traditional policy framework, which is 'presumptive', starts with 'strong preconceptions', produces recommendations in the form of a 'laundry list' of reforms, and is 'biased toward universal recipes', with the new policy approach, which emphasises pragmatism and experimental gradualism. What Rodrik recommends is avoiding 'both market fundamentalism' and 'institutional fundamentalism', and letting each country 'devise its own mix of remedies'.

In a speech delivered in 2005, at a US Federal Reserve event, Indian economist Raghuram Rajan, the then IMF's Chief Economist, warned already at that time about the real possibility of a financial collapse. He argued that, resulting from banks taking higher risks and rewarding with generous compensation such behaviour, there was a probability of severe negative effects. However, for him, the crucial issue remained whether banks would be able to provide liquidity to the financial markets. Based on financial actors' rationality, Rajan pointed to the incentive structure of the financial sector that encouraged this kind of risk (2005: 2–3). In his subsequent 2010 bestseller book *Fault Lines: How Hidden Fractures Still Threaten the World Economy*, Rajan describes the world heading towards the crisis as a world, marked by 'deep fault lines' and excessively dependent on the indebted US consumer to power global economic growth. Easy low-income lending and job-creation policies stemmed, in his view, from the enormous political pressure exercised by the growing inequalities and a weak social safety net.

Olivier Blanchard himself acknowledged the relevance of behavioural economics and behavioural finance, as along with agency theory, when he discussed the workings and incentives of the financial sector (Blanchard 2011). More recently, the works of Thomas Piketty (2013), Angus Deaton (2013), and Joseph Stiglitz (2013) squarely advocated for ways of addressing inequality that do not fit orthodox liberal theories. These economists' ideas on inequality have now currency in Washington circles.

After a long Washington Consensus orthodoxy period, the blossoming of alternatives and the variety of approaches are refreshing, even more so since many of their proponents are part of 'the system', so to speak. It means that even the dominant schools of economic thought are ready to start revising their views. Alternative currents, including evolutionary, institutional, and neo-structuralist economics, have resurfaced.

We are living in exciting times marked by the demise of the ideology that has guided Western policymakers and was imposed on the rest of the world for nearly three decades. In truth, the confluence of the rise of the South along with the decline of the political and ideological supremacy of the West is not accidental. In our current globalised world, the critiques of a prevailing ideology, in particular—derived from post-colonial theories—may be finally expected to emerge from the theoretical isolation of philosophical cultural studies into the open field of political economy.

The unlocking of economic theory and the questioning of disciplinary divisions represent a window of opportunity for reinvigorating an integrated and ambitious sustainable development agenda. The concept of development should be reconsidered through a holistic approach, encapsulating intrinsically linked economic, social, and environmental dimensions, instead of breaking them up into separate compartments. A stronger and more democratic state, supported by efficient governance mechanisms, should assume this role. This is particularly important for public policies to provide better social protection.

Knowledge should become public, in order to promote collective and global creativity. The potential of emerging urban centres could also be used for fostering integrated regional development and planning as well as endogenous participatory decision-making processes (Lopes et al. 2010).

The first practical steps for the actual replacement of the Washington Consensus should focus on recovering the regulatory capacity of the state, aligning national accounting systems to value intangibles, including the incorporation of externalities and the introduction of innovative indicators; guaranteeing basic income; rationalising financial systems of intermediation; redesigning tax systems; adopting budgets that aim at improving the redistribution of resources, according to economic, social, and environmental results; and taxing and registering speculative transactions (Lopes et al. 2010).

This is not the way politics is being practised in the Western world. But the range of heterodox counter-cyclical measures, attempted so far to still address the 2007–2008 crisis, demonstrates the limits of solutions that do not touch the current financial system and the public outcry against unsustained levels of inequality. A brave new world is unfolding before us and Africa needs to be prepared for it by learning from the mistakes of the past while expanding its policy space.

REFERENCES

Addison, T. (2011, June–July). Surprises Ahead? Peering Around the Economic Corner. *WIDER Angle Newsletter*. Helsinki: UNU Wider.

BCG. (2010, June). The African Challengers: Global Competitors Emerge from the Overlooked Continent. *Boston Consulting Group*. Retrieved February 11, 2014, from http://www.bcg.com/documents/file 44610.

Blanchard, O. (2011, March 13). The Future of Macroeconomic Policy: Nine Tentative Conclusions. *iMFdirect*. Retrieved March 20, 2011, from http://blog-imfdirect.imf.org/2011/03/13/future-ofmacroeconomic-policy/.

Chang, H.-J. (2010, November 9). It's Time to Reject the Washington Consensus. *The Guardian*. Retrieved January 6, 2015, from http://www.guardian.co.uk/commentisfree/2010/nov/09/time-to-rejectwashington-seoul-g20.

Deaton, A. (2013). *The Great Escape*. Princeton: Princeton University Press.

Ernst & Young. (2011). *Africa Attractiveness Survey – It's Time for Africa*. Ernst & Young. Retrieved July 7, 2012, from http://www.ey.com/Publication/vwLUAssets/2011_Africa_Attractiveness_Survey/$FILE/Attractiveness_africa_low_resolution_final_WEB.pdf.

Ernst & Young. (2017). *EY's Attractiveness Program Africa*. Retrieved October 12, 2017, from http://www.ey.com/za/en/issues/business-environment/ey-attractiveness-program-africa-2017.

Gaspar, V., & Garcia-Escribano, M. (2017). Inequality: Fiscal Policy Can Make a Difference. *IMF Blog*. Retrieved October 15, 2017, from https://blogs.imf.org/2017/10/11/inequality-fiscal-policy-can-make-the-difference/.

Goes, C. (2016). *Testing Piketty's Hypothesis on the Drivers of Income Inequality: Evidence from a Panel VARs with Heterogeneous Dynamics.* IMF Working Paper, No. 167160, Washington, DC: IMF.

IEO (Independent Evaluation Office of the International Monetary Fund). (2011). *Performance in the Run-Up to the Financial and Economic Crisis. IMF Surveillance in 2004–2007.* Retrieved July 1, 2012, from http://www.ieo-imf. org/ieo/files/completedevaluations/crisis-%20main%20report%20(without%20moises%20signature).pdf.

IMF. (2011). *Enhancing International Monetary Stability—A Role for the SDR?* Retrieved January 23, 2011, from https://www.imf.org/external/np/pp/eng/2011/010711.pdf.

IMF. (2017a). *Debt Sustainability Framework for Low-Income Countries.* Retrieved October 20, 2017, from https://www.imf.org/external/pubs/ft/dsa/lic.htm.

IMF. (2017b). *IMF Conditionality.* Retrieved October 20, 2017, from http://www.imf.org/en/About/Factsheets/Sheets/2016/08/02/21/28/IMF-Conditionality.

Krugman, P. (2008). *International Economics: Theory and Policy.* Mumbai: Pearson.

Krugman, P. (2009, September 6). How Did Economists Get It So Wrong? *New York Times*, MM36. Retrieved January 15, 2010, from http://www.nytimes.com/2009/09/06/magazine/06Economict.html?pagewanted=all.

Lamy, P. (2011, January 24). 'Made in China' Tells Us Little About Global Trade. *Financial Times.* Retrieved January 23, 2011, from http://www.ft.com/cms/s/0/4d37374c-27fd-11e0-8abc-00144feab49a.html#axzz2AXRPPxZ4.

Lin, J. (2012). *The Quest for Prosperity: How Developing Economies Can Take Off.* Princeton, NJ: Princeton University Press.

Lopes, C., Dowbor, L., & Sachs, I. (2010). *Riscos e oportunidades em tempos de mudanças.* São Paulo: Instituto Paulo Freire.

Manuel, T. A. (2003). Africa and the Washington Consensus: Finding the Right Path. *Finance & Development, 40*(3), 18–20, IMF.

McKinsey Global Institute. (2016). *Lions on the Move II: Realizing the Potential of African Economies.* New York: MGI.

Monga, C., & Lin, J. (Eds.). (2015). *The Oxford Handbook of Africa and Economics* (Vol. 2). Oxford: Oxford University Press.

Naim, M. (1999, October 26). *Fads and Fashion in Economic Reforms: Washington Consensus or Washington Confusion.* Working Draft of a Paper Prepared for the IMF Conference on Second Generation Reforms, Washington, DC. Retrieved January 23, 2014, from http://www.imf.org/external/pubs/ft/seminar/1999/reforms/naim.htm.

Ostri, J., Loungani, P., & Davide, F. (2016). Neoliberalism Oversold? *Finance & Development, 53*(2), 38–41, IMF.

Piketty, T. (2013). *Capital in the Twentieth First Century.* Cambridge: Harvard University Press.

Rajan, R. G. (2005, November). *Has Financial Development Made the World Riskier?* NBER Working Paper Series, #11728. Retrieved July 14, 2015, from http://www.nber.org/papers/w11728.

Rajan, R. G. (2010). *Fault Lines: How Hidden Fractures Still Threaten the World Economy.* Princeton, NJ: Princeton University Press.

Rodrik, D. (2011). *The Globalization Paradox.* New York: WW Norton.

Sahn, D. E., Dorosh, P. A., & Younger, S. D. (1997). *Structural Adjustment Reconsidered: Economic Policy and Poverty in Africa.* Cambridge: Cambridge University Press.

Sheil, C., & Stilwell, F. (2017, February 13). The IMF Is Showing Some Hypocrisy on Inequality. *The Conversation.* Retrieved July 14, 2017, from http://theconversation.com/the-imf-is-showing-some-hypocrisy-on-inequality-72497.

Stiglitz, J. (2003). *Globalization and Its Discontents.* New York, London: WW Norton.

Stiglitz, J. (2007). *Making Globalization Work.* New York, London: WW Norton.

Stiglitz, J. (2013). *The Price of Inequality.* New York, London: WW Norton.

Strom, S. (2011, July 4). World Bank's New Tool to Fight Poverty: Its Trove of Data. *International Herald Tribune*, 15.

UNICEF. (1987). *Adjustment with a Human Face* (G. A. Cornia, R. Jolly, & S. Frances, Ed.). Oxford: Clarendon Press.

Whitney, M. (2011, May 19). Dominique Strauss-Kahn Was Trying to Torpedo the Dollar. *Information Clearing House.* Retrieved May 12, 2015, from http://www.informationclearinghouse.info/article28135.htm.

The World Bank. (2017). *Global Investment Competitiveness Report 2017–18.* Washington, DC: World Bank.

CHAPTER 5

Structural Transformation Through Industrialisation

The concept of structural transformation has evolved over time. It has shifted from a simple reallocation of economic activity across three broad sectors (agriculture, industry, and services) that accompanies the process of modern economic growth to encompass issues of sustainability and inclusiveness. I always like to emphasise that structural transformation has been experienced for real by many countries in different regions of the world. But it will not happen spontaneously but probably as a result of deliberate and coherent policies entrenched in a coherent development strategy, enlightened by a transformational leadership.

The principles formulated by Nobel Prize winner Arthur Lewis (1955) are still broadly valid. The focus on increasing productivity though shifting of the economic centre of gravity from agriculture to industry has, nevertheless, taken a beating over the last few years, due to the new expanded value of the services sector, the complexity of globalised value chains, and the acceleration of technological improvements that reduce even further the past centrality of labour costs (Lopes et al. 2017).

Timmer (1986) interprets structural transformation as a process characterised by a decline in the share of agriculture in GDP and employment; a rural-to-urban migration that stimulates the process of urbanisation; a rise in the modern industrial and service economy; and a demographic transition from high to low rates of births and deaths. This requires proactive policies and a strong push from state institutions, coupled with strategic capacity.

© The Author(s) 2019
C. Lopes, *Africa in Transformation*,
https://doi.org/10.1007/978-3-030-01291-5_5

Thomas Theisohn and I published a book in 2003 entitled *Ownership, Leadership and Transformation*, where the issue of understanding the role of national agency was assessed in relation to structural transformation. We argued that traditionally, the notion of capacity came from the engineering world and was understood to involve processes of transferring knowledge (Lopes and Theisohn 2003), especially technical and scientific skills. Little attention was paid to less sector-specific realms, including policy formulation, social and economic research, systems analysis, and review and feedback mechanisms. Today, it is generally accepted that knowledge cannot be simply transferred. It must be acquired, learnt, and reinvented. Additionally, it encompasses both the deep pool of local understanding that is the very foundation of learning and the wealth of global information that can be reconceived to meet local needs (Kararach 2014). This entails a review of the strategic capacities so that the gains being made are not undermined by internal and external threats, including the poor perception of new threats. When adaptation fails to happen, there is no ownership and likely no lasting capacity development.

Structural transformation is perceived by some more in terms of a process by which the relative importance of different sectors and activities of an economy changes over time. Writing about it with my former colleagues at ECA we contend that in the African context, this implies a relative decline of low-productivity agriculture, low value-added extractive activities, and a relative increase in manufacturing and high-productivity services (Lopes et al. 2017; ECA 2013, 2014, 2015, 2016d). This requires proactive policies and strong push from state institutions, coupled with strategic capacity. Developmental macroeconomic policies are also crucial to address the three building blocks of human resources, infrastructure, and institutions. Fiscal, monetary, and financial policies are also key elements of that framework. Despite a stream of 'bad news' Africa is the continent that grows the most. Its debt to GDP ratio has not dramatically changed even in the less favourable 2014–2015 period, and it is negative in relative terms, if reserves are considered. Its macroeconomic profile is more shaken by internal policy blunders that are fixable than by commodity prices per se.

Second, with the current megatrends of rapid urbanisation, the potential of demographic dividends and fast diffusion of information and computer technology are in favour of Africa's transformation. Finally, the continent needs to move from a high-fertility-high-mortality to low-fertility-low-mortality scenario (Lopes et al. 2017; ECA 2013). The argument here is that understanding the role of the African agency and the complexities in this process of transformation is vital.

However, experience shows that there is a strong historical pattern of worsening income distribution between rural and urban economies during the initial stages of the structural transformation—an aspect of the so-called Kuznets' curve (Kuznets 1955). Even currently, rich countries did not escape from this pattern during their early development in the nineteenth and early twentieth centuries. The good news, though, is that absolute poverty does not necessarily worsen during such episodes. In East Asia, for instance, the evidence reveals that absolute poverty fell very rapidly, albeit associated with inequality.

Knowledge of environmental impacts has become more profound, raising the momentum towards a more sustainable and inclusive structural transformation objective that is accompanied by a relative decoupling of resource use and environmental impact from the economic growth process (ECA 2016d). As latecomers to this process, an effective structural transformation for Africans means making significant productivity gains in rural areas with vibrant hubs of agri-business and linkages across industrial activity; the translation of Africa's youth bulge into a demographic dividend; an access to social services that meet minimum standards of quality, regardless of location; reduced inequality—spatial and gender; and a progression towards an inclusive green-growth trajectory (Lopes et al. 2017; Monga and Lin 2015; ECA 2013, 2016d). Africa, therefore, needs to gain an understanding of many urgent and burning questions related to the status, actions, and the method of structural transformation.

Where Is Africa with Respect to Structural Transformation?

Africa, over the past decade, has been remarkably resilient to any global economic volatility. The continent made significant strides during this period in all dimensions of human development, which is comparable with other regions of the world in similar economic trajectories. But such a remarkable performance, despite being often discounted because comparators are not properly used, has not, I have to admit, created enough jobs. Africa remains home to the world's highest proportion of poor people. Furthermore, African economic growth has been proven vulnerable to volatility in commodity prices and demand, and perceptions of fragility.

Despite a continuous stream of renewed pessimism, Africa defies the odds. It is known historically, from the experiences of other regions, that they too faced adversity when they were embarking in their similar industrialisation process (Chang 2002), much like Africa faces now. However, this only contributed to the acceleration of other regions' transformation ambitions, not to slow them down (Lin 2012; Monga and Lin 2015; ECA 2016d). Structural transformation has been operated across regions and historical periods, and Africa as a latecomer has the privilege to learn from others' experience.

Over the period of 1950–1980, Brazil like many countries in Latin America led industrial policy aiming at creating new industrial sectors while changing the prevalent pattern of specialisation in primary commodities and promoting technology-intensive activities (ECA 2016d). As a result, Brazil successfully entered many new industries, such as petrochemical and renewable fuels, especially ethanol, and established foundations for the development of innovation and technology. In the 1980s, the government introduced a more liberal New Industrial Policy package.

In the 2000s, the government targeted specific sectors with Guidelines for Industrial, Technology and Foreign Trade Policy (PITCE). Over the last 30 years, Brazil has been among the most active countries in terms of their use of policies designed to expand industries that process natural resources and are involved in food production. Today, the country is among the top three producers and exporters of orange juice, sugar, coffee, soybean, beef, pork, and chicken. It has also caught up with the traditional big-five grain exporters (the United States, Canada, Australia, Argentina, and the EU).

China has transformed its economic structure through an agro-based industrialisation to accelerate growth and development. The period 1978–1983 emphasised agriculture. In its Five-Year Plan (1981–1985), China encouraged foreign trade and FDI in an attempt to facilitate the importation of advanced technology. Strategic industries identified in the Five-Year Plan of development have been given targeted support such as protection from foreign competition and subsidised loans from state-owned 'policy banks'. Through a deliberate strategy, China has combined a variety of policies to develop both its agricultural and industrial sectors as well as the service one. China became the largest exporter of manufactured goods in two decades.

Another example of successful transformation is the United Arab Emirates (UAE) (ECA 2016c, d). The UAE operated a structural transformation to diversify its economy essentially based on the crude oil sector that accounted for about two-thirds of the GDP. This country developed its industrial base and invested its oil wealth in industry-related infrastructures. Furthermore, in 1985, the first free zone in Dubai, Jebel-Ali, was created with appealing incentives to foreign investments, of which the following were a part: 100% foreign ownership, no custom duties, unlimited repatriation of funds, and exemptions from certain labour laws. The UAE government also promoted a sizable number of manufacturing industries through industrial policy: fertiliser, oil refining, and cement. As of 2010, manufacturing in the UAE accounted for around 10% of GDP, a significant jump from the 0.9% share in 1975 (The World Bank 2013).

Between 1957 and early 1990, Malaysia also achieved substantive economic transformation with its share of manufacturing rising in the GDP from 14% in 1971 to 30% in 1993 (Lall 1995). Malaysia's export to the GDP ratio increased from 46% in 1970 to 95% in 1995 (Athukorala and Menon 1999), and the share of manufacturing in total Malaysian exports rose from 12% to 71% between 1970 and 1993 (Lall 1995). This period had three distinct phases of industrial expansion: import substitution, 1957–1970; New Economic Policy, 1970–1985, the New Development Policy of 1986 that moved the country's industrial policy closer to the type practised by the East Asian newly industrialised economies.

How Should the Continent Deal with Transformation Challenges?

A country's capacity to design and implement a successful transformation agenda can be undermined by internal and external factors. Gains can be reversed if there is inconsistent policy implementation or poor perception of new threats.

Internal factors include poor economic management capacities typified by macroeconomic instability, poor planning design and implementation capacities, weak institutional and individual capacities, limited investments in social and economic infrastructure, limited investment in technology and research and development, and political instability (Lopes 2002). On the other hand, external factors include limited policy space; barriers to trade that undermine export revenues and constrain exports of manufactured goods; the disproportionate concentration on dealing with the official development assistance (ODA) focus areas rather than handling them in their real macrodimension; and the concentration of FDI in the extractive mineral and gas sectors of the economy with limited investments in value-addition. Furthermore, in recent years, climate change has emerged as a threat to development through its destructive impacts.

To address these challenges and promote a sustainable and inclusive structural transformation, the role of institutions and of the state is indispensable (Lin 2012; Lopes et al. 2017; ECA 2013). The emerging consensus is that a developmental state is central to the process of accelerated economic growth and transformation of any country.

The state's role in bailing out the economies in Western countries, following the 2008–2009 global economic crisis, reaffirms the vital role that it can play in sustaining the transformation process. Additionally, it has taken the dust from Keynesian debates. A developmental state is defined as a 'state that puts economic development as the top priority of government policy, and is able to design effective instruments to promote such a goal' (Lopes et al. 2017; ECA 2011). More specifically, a developmental state must deliver a few desired outcomes (ECA 2016a, b):

- Scaling up public investment and public goods provision: Africa, at its stage of development, requires a big push in public investment—economy, region, and continent-wide—in the coming decades. Without committed public investment, sustained private investment will not be made, causing overall productive investment to fall below the level needed to keep the growth momentum going.
- Maintaining macrostability to attract and sustain private investment: In fact, macroeconomic stability is essential, as high uncertainty and risks deter private agents from making forward-looking productive investments. At the same time, harsh fiscal retrenchment and overly restrictive monetary policy aimed at attaining the stabilisation objective alone cannot take the transformation agenda forward.
- Coordinating investment and other development policies: Public investment using scarce resources should be made selectively, sequenced, and directed to achieve the highest development dividends in the long run. This requires public and private investment to be well coordinated across sectors in a big push with aggregate demand spill-overs to facilitate 'a move from a bad to a good equilibrium' (Murphy et al. 1989), especially given the well-known market failure of coordination.

- Mobilising resources and reducing aid dependence over time: This requires a solid framework to develop financial institutions (banking and non-banking) and deepen financial markets.
- Securing fiscal sustainability by establishing fiscal legitimacy: This calls for an urgency to develop the capacity of prudent and efficient public finance management. But this must be the bedrock of a relationship between the government and domestic actors, for fiscal sustainability can be secured only in a medium- to long-period on such a foundation.
- Other development policies critical to structural transformation include trade, technology, financial development, oversight regulation and competition, education and health, and sector-specific policies such as those for industry and agriculture.

As I noted earlier, Africa's recent growth has not generated sufficient jobs and has not been inclusive enough to significantly curb poverty. It has been driven for a third by a commodities price boom and government-related spending. Fluctuations in commodities' prices have made such a growth vulnerable. This reminds us of the imperative for structural transformation that in our case focusses on the potential offered by industrialisation—be it through the expansion of commodity value chains or through the positioning of agro-business to act as the pull factor for agriculture to get out of the doldrums or through the capacity to attract low-value manufacturing production facing rising labour costs in Asia. This is not out of reach (Lin 2012; Severino and Hajdenberg 2016; Chang 2010; AfDB et al. 2011, 2014; ECA 2016d).

The rationale behind much of the current discourse of the 'African Moment' and 'Africa Rising' is clear. Some of the fastest-growing economies in the world are African. Africa has shown relative buoyancy in an era of economic crisis. While the global growth declined after the 2007–2008 crisis, Africa bucked the trend. Notably, all African sub-regions grew at a rate that was faster than the global average in the last decade and a half, with the highest rate being 6.3% and lowest being 3.5%. This remarkable performance was due to several factors, including improved macroeconomic management, increased exports of natural resources, and a growing middle class. Lagos now has a consumer market that is larger than Mumbai's, and the spending power displayed by the continental households exceeds those observed in India and Russia.

This growth experience is, however, not sufficient. It falls way short of the 7% minimum percentage required to double the average income in a decade. This is partly due to the fact that far too many African economies are still dependent on the production and export of primary commodities. Far too many are highly unequal too. Africans are quick to celebrate the fact that seven of its countries are in the top ten in terms of global growth, while they do not mention that a similar number is in the top ten with regard to global inequality. However, one cannot ignore the contradictory reality that despite these figures, far too many Africans remain in the grip of unrelenting hunger and poverty. There is need to look at the complete picture, entailing both successes and setbacks.

An unconventional excursion through Asia allows for interesting comparisons and makes a case for a more benign recognition of the African performance. Although individual conflicts in Asia are known, they are looked at in isolation. Thus, in the Philippines, there are conflicts in Mindanao; in Malaysia, there is the Sabah insurgency; there are border clashes between Thailand and Cambodia; and many others like Myanmar, Sri Lanka, or Nepal. Even rising India suffers from the Naxalite insurgency and the issue of Kashmir, while South Korea sits on the border of a belligerent sister state. If we expand to other parts of Asia including Afghanistan, Pakistan, and West Asia the situation is even worse.

Despite the widespread nature of these conflicts in Asia, the region is still not branded as unstable, but rather seen as a dynamic contributor to global growth. It is true that Africa has conflicts, such as the ones in the Sahel, the Great Lakes Region, Sudan, and Somalia, but these are the remnants of what is now a declining trend of conflict in Africa except for the extremely successful Boko Haram terrorist activities. In other words, though the trend of conflict in Africa is on a downward move and the numbers are smaller than those of Asia, the global perception pertaining to Africa continues to be one of a continent fraught with crisis and the land continues to be viewed as a risky place for making investments.

Two illustrative examples can be presented in this regard. There were about 29 piracy attacks in 2009 off the coast of Somalia as compared to the 150 attacks in the Strait of Malacca in 2005. Yet, this did not lead to generalised negative perceptions about Asia's economic prospects as can be observed in the case of Africa. It should be noted in a similar context, that despite its unstable business environment, Pakistan is the second-largest textile exporter in the world. Thailand with its 19 coups boasts of 12 successful exports and more agricultural products than the whole of sub-Saharan Africa and more manufactured product value than any African country. It, therefore, begs the question of why Africa is still the one to be viewed as conflict-ridden and a seat of political unrest when other countries going through the same problems are not.

Africa desires structural transformation and not structural adjustment, and industrialisation is indispensable to shift the focus of the debate from the domination of a negative to a more positive perception.

If it is accepted that changes will occur when the migration from low to higher productivity takes root in Africa through industrialisation, there is a need for a review of the difficulties for such a path to be adopted.

The push for structural transformation will require a better utilisation of Africa's economic strengths, and it also necessitates all sectors of society, particularly the women and the youth, so they can fulfil their designated roles in the development plan. There is need to perform rigorous analytical thinking in areas of research wherein research can make a difference, such as knowledge of value chains or intellectual property regimes. African states must be supported in their efforts to implement growth-oriented macroeconomic policies and to restore development planning. This will be underpinned by the generation of high-quality data using the latest technologies.

Africa has attempted industrialisation before. In the 1960s and 1970s, newly independent Africa emulated other regions of the world while adopting the model of import-substituting industrialisation. It led to some remarkable progress, but ultimately, it was stymied by the limitations of an approach that involved state-led production rather than state-led facilitation—a model that was marked by the global political economy of the time. This is one more lesson for Africa to be mindful of in the current global context while working on today's industrialisation policies.

In this regard, one approach that bears promising prospects for success is commodity-based industrialisation. Thus, rather than exerting energies on trying to diversify away from commodities, focus must be placed more on using them as effective drivers of industrialisation. In addition to the broader benefits of industrialisation, a commodity-based approach offers immediate scope for value-addition and plenty of opportunity for exploiting forward and backward linkages. Given the dominance of global value chains and intense cost competition in manufacturing trade, Africa can gain an entry into the industrial sector, using its huge commodity and natural resources base. The fact that agro-processing is already one of the most developed manufacturing sectors in the continent is proof that this approach holds enormous potential.

However, achieving success in this regard will not be easy. It will require innovation, skills, and the determination to overcome infrastructural deficiencies. It will require a robust knowledge base of the industry structure and the global value chains. The trading landscape, including barriers and preferences, must be well understood. Above all, boosting intra-Africa trade remains imperative for creating the markets that are needed for successful industrialisation.

MAKING INDUSTRIALISATION THE LOCUS OF NEW DEVELOPMENT STRATEGIES

The high demand for commodities, coupled with their rising prices, has underpinned Africa's growth performance. Given the demographic profile, considerable action is required to diversify production structures into higher employment-intensive activities, as ten million new formal jobs are needed each year to absorb the massive youth population entering the market. African countries must step up and capitalise on recent gains by creating opportunities for social change, including critical human capital investments in education and skill development.

To avoid the negative effects of commodity cycles African countries must focus on policies with the potential to drive inclusive, broad-based growth and development to achieve structural transformation. A major lesson learnt from successful industrial policymaking is that the ruling governments should act as facilitators and enablers (AfDB et al. 2011; McKinsey Global Institute 2016; Lopes et al. 2017).

As African countries prepare to take their place in the future global economy, there is a real opportunity to promote economic transformation through a revamped industrialisation process that is more suited to the realities of Africa. It does so by capitalising on the continent's abundant natural resources, adding value to them, while also introducing measures that will mimic what other regions did in terms of infant industry protection. The evidence from history, right from eighteenth-century Britain to the more recent successful experiences, such as the Republic of Korea, Taiwan, or Singapore, shows that an active industrial policy has been essential for advancing national economic development efforts (Lopes et al. 2017; Chang 2010; McKinsey Global Institute 2010). The spectacular rise of China would not have been possible without the state assuming a developmental role, which is now the subject of immense interest and vast literature.

The manufacturing sector has been the engine of economic development for most of developed countries, and very few countries have managed to develop their economies without a strong manufacturing base, so much so that the terms 'industrialised' and 'developed' are often used interchangeably while referring to a country. In developing such strategies, policies must ensure concomitant investments in infrastructure, human capital, and energy—all of which are critical for expanding the manufacturing sector. ECA estimates that Africa's share in the world manufacturing value-addition has remained very low, standing at 1.5% in 2010, down from 1.9% in 1980. For many African countries, the manufacturing sector will be essential for yielding employment, diversifying technological capabilities that promote and expand the existing skills base, and deepening individual countries' industrial structures.

Expanding the industrial sector will not be easy without stronger regional integration, which provides opportunities for intra-Africa trade. We now know that trade liberalisation prematurely exposed local industries in Africa to unfair competition. There is growing evidence that large sections of the manufacturing sector in Africa have disappeared, owing to underperformance caused by de-linking policy design and implementation, with relevance to the lack of alignment of trade and industrial policies, weak infrastructure and governance, and unfair competition from cheap imported products. There is also empirical data that suggests the pursuit of an African industrial revolution can occur only when large markets drive competitive production and build economies of scale in the context of regional integration.

As latecomers, the conditions under which African countries could advance industrialisation are rather difficult. Their industrial policy measures need to be context-based and address the conditionality's of the 'free market' policy orthodoxy with careful rebranding and refitting. Measures for 'smart specialisation' and capitalisation on regional value chains will facilitate a stronger participation of Africa in the field of global value chains. This would entail addressing supply-side constraints as well as a crafting a business strategy to engage global value chains and the large multinational corporations that dominate them.

Transformative industrial policies (Lopes et al. 2017; Chang 2010; ECA 2016d; AfDB et al. 2011, 2014) present an opportunity for reclaiming the policy space, as the ruling governments can develop industrial policies that build the necessary capabilities that respond to national and regional needs within the confines of global rules. This would call for a systematic review of the current trade and investment policies and agreements, with a view to negotiate or renegotiate such agreements and, wherever possible, manoeuvre through the available flexibilities to ensure that reciprocal control mechanisms are in place. This would entail considering the possibilities of introducing 'smart protectionism' measures—such as the use of tariffs, subsidies, FDI, and other policies at the disposal of African countries. These measures are not directly trade-related and, therefore, are not covered by the World Trade Organization (WTO) or other trade and investment agreements.

In essence, there is a need for a paradigm shift in the application of industrial policymaking, taking lessons from how past experiences have established a unified message and applying mechanisms to support an in-depth understanding of the relevant sectors. There are many opportunities for Africa if the measured frameworks of engagement are put in place to address opportunities and challenges.

All too often, countries adopt a swathe of incentives to promote industrialisation, yet they lack focus. Instead, they usher opaque discretionary and arbitrary practices, insulating inefficiencies and offering rewards without results. Such incentives should not amount to a 'free lunch'. Unfocused policies also mean giving narrow windows of opportunity because of incoherence or slowness.

Africans fought hard to obtain preferential rules of origin for the least developed countries at the Ninth Ministerial Conference of the WTO, held in Bali, Indonesia, in 2013. However, African countries have neither called for the implementation of those preferential criteria in their bilateral negotiations with the EU under the Economic Partnership Agreements, nor have they taken them into account in the African Growth and Opportunity Act that is sponsored by the United States. While engaging in bilateral negotiations with large trading partners, more vigour is necessary. Although the least developed countries had obtained an extension of the transition period for the implementation of the Agreement on Trade-Related Aspects of Intellectual Property Rights, an opportunity for Africa to innovate and promote innovative technologies, this ultimately did not materialise.

With the African economic and political landscape ripe for change, it is incumbent on leaders and the reigning governments to drive industrial policies as part of structural reforms, characterised by Africa's increasingly assertive and vibrant citizenry and private sector. Establishing the right political base requires a government to have an embedded autonomy that invests in solutions rooted in the needs of its society, while having the conviction to execute the 'best fit' policies. The role of the state is, therefore, critical in shaping macroeconomic planning (Lin 2012; Monga and Lin 2015; Lopes et al. 2017; Rodrik 2011; ECA 2011; Clarke and Dercon 2016).

Successful implementation also requires state pragmatism, risk-taking, and constant adaptability to the changing local, regional, and global conditions. Africa's economic and political systems should be internally driven. A prime example of such an approach is the case presented in this report of the Vietnam shipbuilding industry, which, although non-existent in 2002, had become the seventh largest in the world by 2014. Vietnam had developed a detailed plan to develop that industry, including the creation of a state-owned enterprise, providing subsidised loans, retaining corporate tax for reinvestment, exempting export taxes and land rent, increasing local content, and extending loan payments to meet the infrastructure costs of new projects. Such determination shows deliberate policies to affect change, linking the state with the private sector and enhancing backward and forward linkages that can lead the shipbuilding industry to contribute in boosting domestic investment, employment, and output in the transformation process. Africa needs to adopt something on the same line as what has been exemplified above.

Africa needs to overcome its reluctance to undertake the industrial policy (McKinsey Global Institute 2016; Monga and Lin 2015; AfDB et al. 2014). The reluctance has its roots in the mind-set of an era of conditionalities and liberalisation. There is a need for a comprehensive review of the possibilities, highlighting the complexities and shedding light on the debate on selective and general industrial policy. The basic point is this: policy amounts to agency. This entails protecting infant industries while making use of comparative advantages that have long been the focus of industrial policymaking. Africa must identify capacity development and advisory services required for the integration of transformative industrial policies into the national development plans (Lopes et al. 2017).

In fact, industrial policymaking may yield different results and bear different outcomes, like any other kind of policymaking. There is a need to monitor implementation, learn from the experiences of multiple role models, the forerunner, as well as adapt the learnings. Productive industrialisation can come about only if these factors are considered. The question is not whether Africa can industrialise by ignoring its commodities and other resources, but rather how it can use them for value-addition, the introduction of new services, and enhancement of technological capabilities.

RECENT TECHNOLOGICAL DEVELOPMENTS

The debate around structural transformation has tended to focus in the last few years on the possible impact of technological developments in the attractiveness of Africa for industrialisation. Authors like Dani Rodrik (2017) have cast doubts about the possibility of latecomers taking advantage of the cost of labour factor at a time the complexity of value chains and productivity gains do not accommodate latecomers with the same ease as before. According to him:

> manufacturing became a powerful escalator of economic development for low-income countries for three reasons. First, it was relatively easy to absorb technology from abroad and generate high-productivity jobs. Second, manufacturing jobs did not require much skill: farmers could be turned into production workers in factories with little investment in additional training. And, third, manufacturing demand was not constrained by low domestic incomes: production could expand virtually without limit, through exports. (Rodrik 2017)

These three windows of opportunity are closing. Furthermore, some of successful growth stories of the moment are not based on an export-led manufacturing boom replacing exploitation of natural resources. Ethiopia, Côte d'Ivoire, Tanzania, Rwanda, Senegal, or Burkina Faso are all growing at 6%, or higher, without observing all the typical characteristics of the export-led model (Severino and Hajdenberg 2016; Lopes et al. 2017; AfDB et al. 2014).

Manufacturing has become skill-intensive, making it very difficult for latecomers to break into global markets. The move from lower to higher labour productivity in the best performing low-income countries has tended to benefit services rather than manufacturing. In other words, rapid structural change in the said countries has been possible thanks to negative labour productivity growth within non-agricultural sectors (Rodrik 2017). This makes Rodrik conclude that the gains so far may not last or be scalable. The key word is *may*. What Rodrik is introducing is a word of caution given his vast knowledge of the global trade patterns. However, Africa's manufacturing potential should not reside on a traditional export-led model alone.

Africa's growing population and expanding middle class will increase the consumption of processed food significantly. Agri-business is an area where technological advances are easier to absorb and leapfrog. The proximity factor and abundance of natural resources in some countries can be an additional incentive for the establishment of forward and backward linkages that will boost national and close neighbour's value chains. Gains in labour productivity will be linked to the combination of agricultural and industrial opportunities that are closely related to the rapid demographic transformation.

Many pundits believe technological advances will reduce the value of the labour costs' factor to such an extent that low-income countries with high population growth will struggle to catch up (Kelly 2016). The literature is vast with phenomenal predictions about the impact of robotics, automation, and, more recently, artificial intelligence and 3D printing. Such developments combined with health improvements made possible by genomics announce a very different world. Ian Goldin (2016a, b, 2017) talks of a world where technology is contributing to growing inequality across the board, with traditional jobs depending on routine tasks being taken over by computers and robotics in high-income countries. A world of anxieties, shaking the premises of traditional understandings of societal constructs and the political economy. A world where Silicon Valley billionaires advocate for universal basic income, fearing revolt about wage gaps; and the ability of governments to regulate and adjust will deteriorate further.

Africa enters this brave new world unfolding before us with trepidation and understandable fear. I would argue, nevertheless, that innovation and technological developments should not deter the majority of the African countries from pursuing the industrialisation path. I would like to invoke that leapfrogging costs to adjust to new technologies in many domains match the immense retrofitting costs advanced economies will have to incur, particularly for infrastructure in general, and energy in particular. Technologies are making cleaner options cheaper. A vast number of opportunities lie on the frugal utilisation deriving from new discoveries and the quick adaptation of a younger population to change.

The share of higher-productivity sectors as a percentage of GDP is increasing in Africa (Fox et al. 2017), and although this has not dented poverty indicators the way one could hope for, the reality still is that there is a dynamic movement in the right direction. For latecomers the space to increase the share of high productivity in time is considerable. The question of whether there is enough time to do so before being affected by the global technological impacts overhauling of the value chains remains. The space and time dimensions become an essential element for African countries to strategise about and cope with such dramatic developments.

A recent United Nations report on the industrial revolution we are observing demonstrates that very few tasks required for the future would do away completely with human intervention. Existing professions will disappear slowly while new ones will emerge rapidly. The value between the former and the latter will be shifting fast, though. Countries that will prepare for this change in advance will perform better (United Nations 2017). The future of work may be very different from what we are accustomed to but will not be completely devoid of human action.

Technologies are never neutral. In the absence of regulation and standards they may distort social contracts or accepted behaviour patterns. Interventions in the future will require more than government legislation. The roles of institutions will be more diffuse, facing tough legal and political choices (Kelly 2016). Left unchecked disruptions made possible by the new technological developments can contribute to more inequality, ethical challenges, and growing disparities and asymmetries.

REFERENCES

AfDB, OECD, & UNDP. (2011). New Opportunities for African Manufacturing. *African Economic Outlook*. Paris: OECD Publishing.

AfDB, OECD, & UNDP. (2014). Global Value Chains and Africa's Industrialization. *African Economic Outlook*. Paris: OECD Publishing.

Athukorala, P., & Menon, S. (1999). Outward Orientation and Economic Development in Malaysia. *The World Economy, 22*(8), 1119–1139.

Chang, H.-J. (2002). *Kicking Away the Ladder—Development Strategy in Historical Perspective*. London: Anthem Press.

Chang, H.-J. (2010, November 9). It's Time to Reject the Washington Consensus. *The Guardian*. Retrieved January 6, 2015, from http://www.guardian.co.uk/commentisfree/2010/nov/09/time-to-rejectwashington-seoul-g20.

Clarke, D., & Dercon, S. (2016). *Dull Disasters? How Planning Ahead Will Make Difference*. Oxford: Oxford University Press.

ECA. (2011). *Economic Report on Africa: Governing Development in Africa. The Role of the State in Economic Transformation*. Addis Ababa: ECA.

ECA. (2013). *Millennium Development Goals Report 2013: Assessing Progress in Africa Towards the Millennium Development Goals Food Security in Africa – Issues, Challenges and Lessons.* Addis Ababa: ECA.

ECA. (2014). *Economic Report for Africa: Dynamic Industrial Policy in Africa.* Addis Ababa: ECA.

ECA. (2015). *Economic Report on Africa: Industrializing Through Trade.* Addis Ababa: ECA.

ECA. (2016a). *Millennium Development Goals Report 2015: Assessing Progress in Africa Towards the Millennium Development Goals Lessons from the Millennium Development Goals Experience.* Addis Ababa: ECA.

ECA. (2016b). *Economic Report on Africa: Greening Africa's Industrialization.* Addis Ababa: ECA.

ECA. (2016c). *Africa's Blue Economy: A Policy Handbook.* Addis Ababa: ECA.

ECA. (2016d). *Transformative Industrial Policy for Africa.* Addis Ababa: ECA.

Fox, L., Thomas, A., & Haines, C. (2017). *Structural Transformation in Employment and Productivity. What Can Africa Hope for?* Washington, DC: IMF.

Goldin, I. (2016a). *The Pursuit of Development.* Oxford: Oxford University Press.

Goldin, I. (Ed.). (2016b). *Is the Planet Full?* Oxford: Oxford University Press.

Goldin, I. (2017). The Second Renaissance. *Nature, 550*(7676), 327–329.

Kararach, G. (2014). *Development Policy in Africa: Mastering the Future?* Basingstoke: Palgrave Macmillan.

Kelly, K. (2016). *The Investable. Understanding the 12 Technological Forces That Will Shape Our Future.* New York: Viking.

Kuznets, S. (1955). Economic Growth and Income Inequality. *American Economic Review, 49*(1), 1–28.

Lall, S. (1995). Industrial Strategies and Policies on Foreign Direct Investment in East Asia. *Transnational Corporations, 4*(3), 1–26.

Lewis, A. (1955). *The Theory of Economic Growth.* Chicago: R. D. Irwin.

Lin, J. (2012). *The Quest for Prosperity: How Developing Economies Can Take Off.* Princeton, NJ: Princeton University Press.

Lopes, J. C. (2002). *J. Amaral, J. Dias, External Dependency, Value-Added Creation and Structural Change: The Input-Output Linkage Approach Revisited.* Retrieved February 20, 2017, from https://www.researchgate.net/publication/5130114_External_dependency_value-added_creation_and_structural_change_the_input-output_linkage_approach_revisited.

Lopes, C., & Theisohn, T. (2003). *Ownership, Leadership and Transformation.* New York, London: UNDP and Earthscan.

Lopes, C., Hamdock, A., & Elhiraika, A. (Eds.). (2017). *Macroeconomic Policy Framework for Africa's Structural Transformation.* London: Palgrave Macmillan.

McKinsey Global Institute. (2010). *Lions on the Move.* London, New York: MGI.

McKinsey Global Institute. (2016). *Lions on the Move II*. London, New York: MGI.

Monga, C., & Lin, J. (Eds.). (2015). *The Oxford Handbook of Africa and Economics* (Vol. 2). Oxford: Oxford University Press.

Murphy, K., Shleifer, A., & Vishny, R. W. (1989, October). Industrialization and the Big Push. *Journal of Political Economy, 97*(5), 1003–1026.

Rodrik, D. (2011). *The Globalization Paradox*. New York: WW Norton.

Rodrik, D. (2017). Growth Without Industrialization? *Project Syndicate*. Retrieved October 20, 2017, from https://www.project-syndicate.org/commentary/poor-economies-growing-without-industrializing-by-dani-rodrik-2017-10.

Severino, J.-M., & Hajdenberg, J. (2016). *Entreprenante Afrique*. Paris: Odile Jacob.

Timmer, C. P. (1986). *The Agriculture Transformation*. Cambridge: Harvard Institute of International Development, Harvard University.

United Nations. (2017). *Frontier Issues: The Impact of Technological Revolution on Labour Markets and Income Distribution*. New York: United Nations.

The World Bank. (2013). *Growing Africa: Unlocking the Potential of Agribusiness*. Washington, DC: World Bank.

CHAPTER 6

Increasing Agricultural Productivity

I have tried to demonstrate that agriculture as a sector is not to be treated as if it was de-linked from the call for industrialisation. I have often face decision-makers in the continent concerned about agriculture and its importance for the wellbeing of vast number of people reject the centrality of industrialisation. This is due to poor understanding of the relationship between the two.

Agriculture has driven economic growth in countries across the globe for centuries. It has played a key role in bringing about economic transformation and the industrialisation of economies in Europe, America, and Asia. In this respect, the most prominent pattern observed in instances of modern development is the secular decline in agriculture's share in the GDP along with the consequent increase in the combined shares of industry and services in the structure of successfully transformed economies.

Accounting for almost 65% of Africa's employment and 75% of its domestic trade, agriculture is likely to continue influencing the continent's economic growth for years to come (Monga and Lin 2015; Severino and Hajdenberg 2016; Lopes et al. 2017; ECA 2013a, 2014). Smallholder farmers will be the backbone of this effort. Emerging markets, either within or outside Africa, hold the promise of greater profits for smallholder farmers. Feeding the rapidly growing urban population and middle class will generate higher demand for quality agricultural and processed food products. Value added to farmers' outputs has the potential to increase the net income generation for years.

© The Author(s) 2019
C. Lopes, *Africa in Transformation*,
https://doi.org/10.1007/978-3-030-01291-5_6

A key first step in transforming African agriculture is to increase productivity coming from commercial, rather than subsistence, activities. Most smallholder farmers in Africa are neither productive nor profitable. There are two significant reasons why they remain trapped in the cycle of subsistence.

First, their outputs are too low in terms of quantity as well as quality to generate marketable surpluses, because, for the most part, they lack access to modern technology and production-enhancing inputs.

Second, farmers are disconnected from output markets. Poor infrastructure makes linkages between farm-level production and downstream activities, such as processing and marketing, almost impossible (AUC and ECA 2009). Given that approximately 65% of Africans rely on agriculture as their primary source of livelihood and despite the wide variety of crops, animals, and farm practices across the continent (ECA 2013b), it is no surprise that Africa has the lowest levels of agricultural productivity in the world.

While land productivity in India has grown from 0.95 tons per hectare to 2.53 tons per hectare over the past 50 years, Africa's land productivity is stuck at 1.5 tons per hectare. This statistic persists despite agricultural land being three to six times more available in Africa than in countries like China and India, both of which, despite having much lower available agricultural land per capita (at 0.6 hectare for China or 0.3 hectare for India), have successfully managed to secure food for their 'bottom billion'.

Africa, on the other hand, with its immense natural resources, is the world's most food-insecure region. Around 227 million people, or one out of every five people, in Africa are chronically food insecure. In fact, compared to the rest of the world, while Africa houses around 15% of the world's population, it is home to close to a third of those affected by hunger on our planet. During these challenges, however, there is no doubt that agriculture in Africa has also had some success stories (Fox et al. 2017; Rodrik 2017).

The interventions of the Ghana government to introduce mechanised farming systems and make block farming a reality for small-scale farmers have successfully turned the country into an established food basket. In Uganda, the production of fish has dramatically increased by 35% over the last decade, resulting in aquaculture production, rising from 285 metric tons in 1999 to over 100,000 metric tons today. Egypt's rice yield today stands at 9 metric tons per hectare, making this the best rice output in the world. Its rice production was expected to reach around 7.5 million tons in 2014, amounting to earnings of about half a billion dollars. Water harvesting in Tanzania has been successfully scaled up in the lowlands, where seasonal rainfall can amount to as much as 600 to 900 mm, improving the Majaluba rain-fed rice farms. With the help of low-cost individual pump schemes, Nigerian farmers have turned to small-scale irrigation by using shallow groundwater recharged by the river and lifting it with the *shadouf* or *calabash* in the dry season to grow vegetables for city dwellers.

The successes mentioned above are still too sparse and do not reflect a consistent quest for higher productivity. Most African farmers have not benefitted from initiatives and programmes aimed at improving farming techniques, farm equipment, seeds, fertilisers, post-harvest technology, agricultural financing, and so on.

WHY HAS SUCCESS REMAINED ELUSIVE?

The simple response is that agriculture, the sector that seems to hold one of the key solutions for the continent's transformation-related problems, has long been neglected and ill-guided. This is reflected by the fact that spending, either public expenditure or what is used for ODA, has largely been improperly allocated while not addressing fundamental economic requirements. For example, in 2002, Africa received almost double the amount of ODA for agriculture (US $713.6 million) than what was given to the countries of Eastern and Southeast Asia (US $479.8 million). This did not, however, translate into greater returns for the extra dollar. African countries' expenditure on agriculture has always been, with few exceptions, less than the CAADP budgetary target of 10% (NEPAD 2010).

History tells us that nations that have succeeded in bringing their people out of poverty have done it on the dint of an agricultural revolution that involved systematic improvements in production, storage, processing, distribution, and usage. Increase in agricultural productivity has, from the time of the European industrial revolution, contributed immensely to fast-tracking the structural transformation of their economies. Notable examples of the effect of the agricultural revolution on the economies of Brazil, India, and China show how these countries used the surplus from increased agricultural productivity to fuel their growth models.

Africa's agriculture is yet to be used as a true tool for transformation. Africa has within its reach the capacity, resources, and opportunities to lead the way to sustainable development. There are several prerequisites for a coherent policy drive towards attaining a truly transformed agricultural sector.

Throughout, this chapter emphasises agriculture as the main engine of sustained growth and posits that its successful transformation is imperative to achieve inclusive and sustained rural and overall economic transformation. The words of Timmer (2005: 3) on the subject are as follows:

> No country has been able to sustain a rapid transition out of poverty without raising productivity in its agricultural sector. … The process involves a successful structural transformation where agriculture, through higher productivity, provides food, labour, and even savings to the process of urbanisation and industrialisation.

Therefore, in this chapter successful agricultural transformation refers to a development in the agriculture sector that is associated with the occurrence of the two following simultaneous developments:

- Productivity (output per unit of input, variously defined) increases, sustained over two to three decades at least
- Sustained income increases for most of the farmers and rural households

Therefore, there is a need to search for evidence of the existence and extent of these two developments, to gain a better understanding of Africa's current agricultural transformation path.

Africa's Performance in the Primary Sector

Agricultural transformation in Africa has accelerated remarkably since 1990, as indicated by underlining indicators—for example, agricultural productivity, cereal yield, and per capita agricultural income. Most countries doubled their average rates of transformation, following the launch of CAADP in 2003. Specifically, Africa has, on average, witnessed an increase of agricultural productivity, measured as agricultural value-added per agricultural worker, of around 67% during the period between 1990 and 2012. However, the overall performance marks significant variation among countries, in terms of both the level of productivity and the pace of progress. As far as the pace of growth is concerned, while some countries have succeeded in increasing productivity by a whopping 326% (Nigeria), others have experienced a decline in the order of 45% (Burundi). In general, out of the 48 African countries for which data is available, 18 countries have managed to increase labour productivity by more than 50% during the period 1990–2012, 16 countries by 1 to 49.9%, and 14 countries have witnessed a decline by 45%. However, it should be noted that African countries have, in general, witnessed a significant increase in labour productivity over the last decade and a half when compared with the earlier period.

Compared to some other regions of the world, Africa's performance is, nevertheless, modest. East Asia and the Pacific (developing countries only), Latin America and the Caribbean (developing countries only), Europe, and China have experienced increases in labour productivity of 115%, 72%, 130%, and 133% respectively during the same period of interest. Overall progress masks significant variation across the main subregions in Africa. While North Africa's average productivity grew by 64%, the rest of Africa witnessed, on an average, an acceleration of 52% in 1990–2012.

African countries exhibit a wide variation in registered productivity levels, ranging from as low as US $129 per worker in Burundi to as high as US $8155 per worker in Mauritius, as observed in 2012.

Reflecting the increase in agricultural productivity, cereal yield was, on average, consistently growing at an annual average rate of 1.17% during the period 1990–2013 from 1194 to 1531 kg per hectare. Africa, in general, has been moving faster in 2003–2013, at an average annual change of 13 kg, compared to the 11 kg witnessed during 1990–2002. The progress registered in cereal yield in Africa since 1990, which is 28%, is, however, extremely modest compared to that of other regions.

Despite progress, Africa's average cereal yield remains by far the lowest in the world, representing 40% of the world's average cereal yield. It has slightly declined from 42% since 1990. There is an immense potential to at least double or even triple the cereal yield.

African countries' performance varies significantly when measured through their cereal yield output. The progress achieved rate ranges between 70% (São Tomé and Príncipe) and a spectacular 175% (Côte d'Ivoire), with eight countries registering a growth of more than 101% and ten countries experiencing a growth of 63–96% through the period between 1990 and 2013.

In relation to yield level, African countries can be classified into three categories. A category of premier achievers (22 countries) with a yield level that is mostly well above Africa's average yield. The second group of countries which consists of 13 countries that register a yield level lower than Africa's average yield but above 1000 kg per hectare. The third group includes 16 countries with an inferior yield level of less than 1000 kg per hectare. Interestingly and sadly, those 16 countries are among a list of 18 countries with the world's lowest cereal efficiency (with the cereal yield of 1000 kg per hectare or less).

It must be considered that no African country, except for Egypt, has managed to post a cereal yield that is above or even equal to the world's average. Côte d'Ivoire's remarkable achievement should be highlighted in this context. It has managed to boost its yield by a whopping 175% in 1990, from a low yield of 1112 kg per hectare to around 3054 kg per hectare. This registers Africa's fourth-highest cereal yield, which is only behind Egypt, South Africa, and Mauritius. The high cereal yield in Côte d'Ivoire could be partially attributed to the significant improvement achieved in labour productivity, estimated at 47% during 1990–2008. The high productivity realised in Côte d'Ivoire has contributed to boosting impressive growth in the production of major crops. Yam production has increased by 124% during 1990–2013. Cocoa and plantains have witnessed an increase of 104% and 33% between 1990 and 2012 respectively, while cashew nut crops experienced a growth of 1131% during 1997–2012. Additionally, 11 African countries experienced a consistent decline in cereal yield over 1990–2013, a trend that certainly merits an in-depth analysis (author's calculations based on The World Bank 2013).

Reflecting on the sustained income dimension of agricultural transformation, the average value of food production is used as a proxy for rural income. Africa has experienced a steady increase of this average. Progress substantially accelerated after 2003, posting an average annual increment to US $1.44 from a mere US $0.17 during the period 1990–2002. However, despite this encouraging progress, Africa fared low in terms of food production and income compared to other developing countries.

Malawi's and Angola's remarkable rise in cereal yield of 109% and 162% respectively in 1990–2012 is worth noting. On the other hand, Côte d'Ivoire, Africa's most aggressive performer in cereal yield improvement, with a total growth of 175% during the same period, achieved a modest growth in average food value by only 8%. With this rapid return to agricultural success (a possible second agro-business miracle and industrial take-off, after a decade-long electoral and political crisis), this agri-business success in Côte d'Ivoire shows that successful agriculture transformation is possible in the context of a small-sized country as well.

MODERNISING SMALL-SCALE AGRICULTURE

Once one gets a clear picture of Africa's agricultural performance, the need becomes evident to innovate in terms of ideas, transformation models, new products, and innovation platforms to meet the most difficult challenges and compete successfully in all areas, including agriculture, by putting the last at the first position with an effective reverse pyramid-base strategy. Smallholders dependent on nature and weather can no longer feature as the main source of African agricultural output in the era of a knowledge-based world economy. Policymakers have facilitated political discussions, but the reality remains that subsistence farming on small plots of land, still characterised by extremely low productivity and surpluses, is the dominant mode of agricultural production in the continent, as compared to the importance it held 25 years ago (ECA 2013b).

A major reason why agriculture in Africa has remained in the subsistence form is that smallholders, who contribute to around 80% of Africa's agricultural production, have been overlooked and marginalised in the process of value chain development. For smallholders to grow, they will need to understand how they are interrelated to national, regional, continental, and international consumers.

Understanding the global value chain of a product when it leaves the farm gate is one of the missing links. Consequently, the need to operate in the value chain as a partner and contributor is critical. The benefits for the farmer's participation are not solely limited to increased productivity. The demand for products will generate, at the farm level, additional use of fertilisers, use of improved seeds, and more appropriate, efficient, and adapted agricultural practice and technologies. Thus, the smallholder needs to be connected to input markets. More importantly, smallholders suffer from marginalisation of inputs and value chain inclusion. This is compounded by the fact that agriculture itself is generally considered to be a non-profitable and risky sector at the smallholder level. Modernisation is perceived as something that lies in the department of big entrepreneurs, who have access to capital and financial institutions (ECA 2013a; NEPAD 2013).

To resolve such a stumbling block, how then can the smallholder access financing? Most rural areas, where smallholder farmers are located, have no or limited networks of financial institutions. Even where these exist, smallholder farmers, with poor credit ratings and sometimes with no collateral-like title deeds, cannot compete in obtaining financial resources and are excluded when it comes to technicalities. Commercial banks in Africa avoid agriculture based on the perceived risk. In addition, most commercial banks are normally located in urban areas, preventing their ready accessibility to farmers. When they are indeed located in rural areas, it is to collect cash deposits and savings from farmers, providing little assistance or financial innovation opportunities.

Many African countries are now establishing 'Agricultural Development Banks' and setting out policies and strategies reinforced by agricultural finance products to assist smallholder farmers, especially women farmers to facilitate their access to credit and finance for their entrepreneurial activities as well as to include them in value chains. Financial services to smallholder farmers play a strong and pervasive role that affects not just the farmers but the entire economy and society in general.

Access to credit puts smallholder farmers on the road to expansion and growth through more productive and efficient methods of production, harvest, storage, and distribution. While a lot of progress has been made in easing access, smallholder farmers still have very limited access to appropriate financing. Further gains in productivity cannot be achieved without increasing the agricultural income of smallholder farmers and creating rural farm employment opportunities (Tsakok 2011; Acemoglu and Robinson 2012). This would require linking smallholder farmers to each of the input and product markets. More importantly, smallholder farmers need to benefit from greater value-addition to their products so that they can break away from subsistence farming and create more value while retaining much of the wealth created (AUC and ECA 2009; ECA 2013a; Acemoglu and Robinson 2012).

Wealth creation in Africa can find impetus from the agriculture sector. Given that most smallholders in Africa are women, they are often barred from the usual credit channels. They are left with micro-credit institutions or NGOs that do not have the financial depth to make agriculture an enabler of growth and a wealth-creation opportunity. To advance the agenda of strengthening value chains for increased food production, it is a prerequisite to consider the role of women in farming. The limited access to credit revolves around the high-risk rating of smallholder farming as an agricultural sector, added to inverse economies of scale and related low profitability of lending to this market segment.

Many instruments have been designed and customised to address this issue. In terms of products, both group and individual loans have been successfully used—with group loans reporting better loan portfolio quality than individual lending approaches in a number of countries in Africa. To achieve inclusive agriculture value chain financing, there is a need to map successful smallholder financing schemes in the continent, as a starting point, in order to change the discourse of investment in agriculture (Severino and Hajdenberg 2016; McKinsey Global Institute 2016; AUC and ECA 2009).

FOOD INSECURITY

The next hurdle that needs to be resolved on the path to optimising the agricultural sector is the one posed by food insecurity (AfDB et al. 2013). In Africa, estimates show a dramatic increase in the number of people experiencing chronic hunger through the period 1990–2007 and a steeper one following the 2008–2009 financial and economic crises (ECA 2013c). Political instability, wars, harsh weather, and the lack of incentives for agricultural transformation have played a significant role in compounding food insecurity in Africa. Food and agricultural production and productivity have barely improved (except in a few cases), and other critical elements, such as intersectoral linkages to other economic activities and diversification in staple production, are also lacking. Rapid population growth and climate change continue to negatively impact food security, and they need to be factored into sustainable strategies and policies. The political and social uprisings in North Africa and West Africa have increased household food insecurity, displaced thousands of people, and affected local economies. Frequent droughts in the Horn of Africa and the Sahel have persisted, leaving millions of people destitute.

Recent estimates of the Global Hunger Index (GHI), which is estimated for 122 countries, show that during the period 1990–2012, across regions and countries, GHI scores vary greatly with the highest GHI scores occurring in South Asia and sub-Saharan Africa. South Asia reduced its GHI score substantially between 1990 and 1996. Though sub-Saharan Africa made less progress than South Asia after 1990, it has caught up since the turn of the millennium. The GHI score for sub-Saharan Africa fell by 16%, which is much less than what was observed in South Asia (26%), Middle East, and North Africa (35%). Although 31 countries in Africa improved their GHI score during this period, only two countries in Africa—Ghana and Egypt—are ranked among the ten best performers.

In terms of absolute progress, however (while comparing the 1990 and the 2014 GHI), six of the world's ten best performing countries, experiencing the biggest improvements in scores, are in Africa. Yet, most of the world's 16 countries where the level of hunger is either 'extremely alarming' or 'alarming', according to 2014 GHI scores, are also in Africa. With the exception of Iraq all the countries in which the hunger situation worsened from the 1990 GHI to the 2014 GHI are in the sub-Saharan Africa. Increased hunger since 1990 in some of these countries can be readily attributed to prolonged conflict and political instability (von Grebmer et al. 2014; IFPRI 2013). Available estimates show that about 25% of Africa's population, around 245 million persons, do not have sufficient access to food to meet even their basic nutritional needs and about 30–40% of children under the age of five suffer from chronic malnutrition. Some countries, such as Ethiopia or Angola, have made real progress in the fight against hunger.

Challenges remain for most countries, especially in East Africa, a subregion that was a host to 73% of the estimated total number of hungry people in Africa, over the period 2006–2008. Any substantial progress in this sub-region and in the Sahel would have an important impact on the containment of hunger in Africa.

Rapid population growth, compounded by a massive reflux of refugees, is another major aggravating factor leading to hunger in Africa. These factors hinder progress in achieving the hunger reduction target established by the World Food Summit (WFS) in countries such as Rwanda, Ethiopia, and Tanzania that had the largest and fastest reductions in the proportion of undernourishment.

By engaging in a coherent and strategic transformation policy, Africa can shift the debate to securing an African value chain for current and future generations, which is connected to the global value chain (AUC and ECA 2009; AfDB et al. 2014). An important shift in the perception of agriculture is underway as a majority of African governments no longer understand agriculture as a way of life for farmers but as an economic activity with real and tangible benefits for the transformation of the country concerned (ECA 2014).

Agriculture being a catalyst for economic transformation may become clear for a considerable number of African countries if it is enhanced with capital investment, agricultural research and technology, yield-enhancing practices and technologies, land distributive policies, labour productivity, and market access and infrastructure.

NEED FOR AGRI-BUSINESS

I have already presented some of the arguments as to why to create and sustain wealth and production in the long run, Africa's natural resources, including rich agriculture-related resources, should be transformed into higher forms of capital, preferably tradable industries (AUC and ECA 2014). This involves giving priority to economic development, expanding production and value-addition, and responding to the increased demand for a more sophisticated consumption of goods.

There is a strong consensus that an expanding and prosperous productive economy is crucial for the structural transformation of African economies, and it is the only sustainable pathway out of poverty and hunger. Making productive and valuable use of natural resources and upgrading primary products can help resolve some of the continent's challenges, including poverty and food insecurity. This could inspire a virtuous circle of higher output through intensive technology and innovation, elevated national productivity, higher average incomes, and superior and inclusive prosperity.

Historically, the pathway out of poverty for most communities and countries has been through a sustained structural transformation process. This pathway involves higher labour productivity in the overall economy, convergence in terms of labour productivity between agriculture and non-agriculture sectors, and realisation of intensive value-addition activities. Indeed, high agricultural productivity is essential for economic transformation that is based on reducing the relative share of agricultural output and labour in favour of other productive sectors including industrialisation at large (Tsakok 2011; ECA 2013a; AUC and ECA 2014).

It is well observed that countries with low agricultural productivity tend to be less industrialised and, therefore, are located at earlier stages on the development ladder. This could be attributed to the fact that agriculture is the main source of raw material (or surplus) needed for industrialisation, labour to be relocated to other emerging economic activities, and remittances to other productive activities. In addition, it is a major market for the outputs of other sectors.

Despite the recognised role agriculture could play in unlocking the continent's true potential (by turning agriculture into a business), the sector has remained hampered by a number of well-documented constraints and bottlenecks that must be overcome to get agri-business back on track and moving (ECA 2013a; Brenton 2012; Deininger et al. 2011; The World Bank 2007, 2010).

Considering the wide diversity of the African agriculture context, it may help to mention the most identified categories of challenges faced by African agri-business operators before taking on specific constraints that are commonly reported within the value chains in select fast-transforming economies (Nigeria, Kenya, Côte d'Ivoire, Ghana, Senegal, Zambia, to name a few), whose ongoing transformative agri-business experiences mirror much of what the rest of Africa must also overcome.

Based on the evidence, the categories of real or perceived problems affecting output as well as input markets across value chains include the lack of innovation, inadequate policy, legal and regulatory constraints, infrastructure and logistical bottlenecks, financial constraints, market access, information and knowledge limitations, quality standards and hygiene standards that are not up to mark, production inputs, and scarcity of raw materials.

These forward a snapshot of a range of the well-known generic challenges and constraints encountered over time across systems and countries and those that are still not well addressed to date. A good case in point is the problems faced by the agri-business community in Nigeria. As can be noted in the results of a survey carried out to identify the perceived problems hindering the successful operation and efficient running of agri-business firms in Nigeria, the range of difficulties includes low level of technology, low investment, prohibitive cost of production, macroeconomy-related problems, poor-performing infrastructure, unpredictable government planning, poor access to markets, inadequate access to finance, weak legal systems, and poor returns on investments.

These hurdles are translated into myriad inefficiencies and losses in Nigeria, including post-harvest losses for cereals, roots and tuber, fruits and vegetables. Beyond the issue of the economies of scale and means, which should not be overlooked, the agri-business challenges remain daunting when considered from the perspective of the firm size. In a survey carried out in Ghana in the first quarter of 2011, in order to gauge the business sentiment of Chief Executive Officers from the Association of Ghana Industries, similar findings confirmed the size of the challenge. As can be learnt from these cases, it appears clear that the true solutions to Africa's agriculture and agri-business problems are well beyond the scale or means of a single country.

LABOUR DYNAMICS AND URBANISATION

Historically, successful economic development has been stimulated and sustained by the rising productivity of agricultural labour. Evidence suggests that agricultural labour productivity plays a key role within wider economic transformation processes. Therefore, agricultural revolutions that enhance agricultural labour productivity in poor agrarian economies can contribute significantly to economic transformation by playing multiple foundational roles in the wider development processes (AfDB et al. 2015; ECA 2017).

Increased labour productivity leads to improving food availability per unit of labour. First it reduces the cost and, consequently, the price of food relative to agricultural workers' incomes, which, in turn, increases agricultural workers' budget surpluses and, hence, increases their real incomes. It then stimulates the demand for non-food goods and services and concurrently releases agricultural labour from agricultural production to non-agricultural production, consequently spurring economic growth and development. Later industrial, services, and knowledge revolutions would build on the increase in supply and demand for non-food goods and services to reduce their prices by lowering labour costs and reaping benefits from the economies of scale. One should expect that the potential benefits from increased agricultural labour productivity would then drop. This is associated with increase in the relative importance of industrial services and knowledge in raising the productivity of an increasing volume of labour, involved in the production of non-agricultural goods and services.

In 1980, around 28% of Africans lived in cities, as compared to around 40% in 2010. It is now projected that over 50% of Africa's population will live in cities by 2020. This phenomenon that theoretically reduces the burden on agriculture to support the livelihood of millions of rural dwellers will increase the pressure on agriculture to meet the growing food consumption associated with a dramatic change in patterns. On the other hand, urbanisation should contribute to increasing demand, investment, and productivity with workers moving from historically low-productive agriculture to what are widely perceived as high-productive urban jobs.

Shifts from rural-to-urban employment was found to contribute around 20–50% of productivity growth in a number of countries, depending on the level of productivity achieved in both agricultural and non-agricultural sectors.

Urbanisation, if coupled with the construction of more infrastructural elements, such as roads, water, and sewage systems, is vital to absorb the additional 600 million people set to enter Africa's labour force by 2040, which would be more than what is observed in both China and India. The impact of an expanding labour force on the GDP in Africa is tremendous, generating an increase of around 75% of GDP per capita over the last 25 years, as compared to the 25%, which came from higher labour productivity associated with urban jobs. The challenge in this regard is for Africa to ensure that urbanisation is not coupled with just creating slums and to provide young generations with the skills required to turn the anticipated large workforce into a major engine for development. Figures from 2012 show that 87% of African food items imports were from outside the continent, whereas developing Asian economies imported 34% of agricultural raw materials from their region, and the proportion for European countries stands at 63% from their region (AUC and ECA 2014).

African economic growth has, in the past, been substantially fuelled by primary commodity exports. The consequences of counting on a commodity-driven growth path have been mentioned. These consequences can be evaded by adopting an agri-business growth strategy that fits both the resource endowment of most African economies and the conditions surrounding the overwhelming majority of the poor who live in rural areas and depend on agriculture for their livelihood. Agri-business is substantially labour-intensive in terms of creating jobs and generating forward and backward linkages in the value chain.

The need for agri-business development rather than agriculture-led development is real. This should entail a paradigm shift from a supply to a demand-driven market, in which the agri-business value chain, covering agriculture, industry, and services, plays an essential role (Lopes et al. 2017; Yumkella et al. 2012).

First, there is a need to reemphasise upon strategies and policies aimed at structural agricultural transformation. For an integrated approach that encompasses economic, social, and environmental dimensions, we need to focus on food, land, water, forest security, bio-energy resources, urban and rural as well as forward and backward linkages between agriculture and other evolving sectors of African economies. This is how agri-business can be turned into a major source of wealth creation.

Second, there is a need to reduce the vulnerability of millions of African small-scale farmers and consumers to high, volatile prices, while increasing their resilience to shocks. The misconception of food security as a replacement for poverty reduction must be debunked. Food security should be approached economically and not as a poverty-reduction programme.

Third, while recognising that Africa's industrialisation must count on its commodities, the case needs to be made to undertake the same while addressing global climate change. Value-addition should take place close to where the resources are, thereby reducing large carbon footprints that come with transporting commodities over wide distances for processing. Africa must see itself also as a key player in solving climate change issues, rather than a victim of the same. With the largest reservoir of unused arable land, it is still the natural leader in a food-insufficient world. Not being locked into any technology preferences allows it to leapfrog to green and clean energy, which is boosted by the best potential found in this area that Africa boasts of in the world. Africa must become a price-maker and not the price-taker, particularly when it has a controlling size that sets commodity trends.

Finally, Africa must remain firm against unfair trade policies and protocols. For example, agricultural subsidies in developed countries continue to distort international commodity markets and lead to dumping, depressing prices. As a result, this makes agriculture unprofitable for African smallholder farmers. The deal between cocoa processors, Cargill and Archer Daniels Midlands, has allowed the new company to control around 60% of the total world trade in cocoa. Paradoxically, two African countries, Côte d'Ivoire and Ghana, produce 60% of the cocoa worldwide. The end result is palpable already. In Côte d'Ivoire, cocoa producers are experiencing a downfall in price. The quasi-monopoly of two countries on one commodity has not been translated into strategic bargaining and trade performance. In contrast, the Bali WTO agreement demonstrated the strength displayed by India, with a smaller economy than Africa, when it came to defend the interests of its agricultural sector.

The simple reading of the demonstrations above is that the agricultural sector has shown in the past that it can sparkle sweeping changes in the growth of a nation. However, there are stumbling blocks, such as poor infrastructure and low financing as well as wrong policy focus and incentives that hinder such potential. By resolving these issues, the sector higher productivity bears a lot of promise for the transformational change that Africa requires.

REFERENCES

Acemoglu, D., & Robinson, J. (2012). *Why Nations Fail: The Origins of Power, Prosperity, and Poverty.* New York: Crown Publishers.

AfDB, OECD, & UNDP. (2013). Structural Transformation and Natural Resources. *African Economic Outlook.* Paris: OECD Publishing.

AfDB, OECD, & UNDP. (2014). Global Value Chains and Africa's Industrialization. *African Economic Outlook.* Paris: OECD Publishing.

AfDB, OECD, & UNDP. (2015). Regional Development and Spatial Inclusion. *African Economic Outlook.* Paris: OECD Publishing.

AUC, & ECA. (2009). *Economic Report on Africa, Developing African Agriculture Through Regional Value Chains.* Addis Ababa: ECA.

AUC, & ECA. (2014). *Transforming Africa's Agriculture for Shared Prosperity and Improved Livelihoods Through Harnessing Opportunities for Inclusive Growth and Sustainable Development.* Synthesis Paper on the Theme of Agriculture and Food Security, Prepared for Assembly of the Africa Union, 33rd Ordinary Session, Heads of State and Government Summit.

Brenton, P. (2012). *Africa Can Help Feed Africa: Removing Barriers to Regional Trade in Food Staples.* Washington, DC: World Bank.

Deininger, K., Byerlee, D., Lindsay, J., Norton, A., Selod, H., & Stickler, M. (2011). Rising Global Interest in Farmland: Can It Yield Sustainable and Equitable Benefits? In *Agriculture and Rural Development.* Washington, DC: World Bank.

ECA. (2013a). *Millennium Development Goals Report 2013: Assessing Progress in Africa Towards the Millennium Development Goals Food Security in Africa – Issues, Challenges and Lessons.* Addis Ababa: ECA.

ECA. (2013b). *Rethinking Agricultural and Rural Transformation in Africa. Challenges, Opportunities and Strategic Policy Options.* Addis Ababa: ECA, Mimeo.

ECA. (2013c). *Status of Food Security in Africa: A Parliamentary Document.* Addis Ababa: ECA.

ECA. (2014). *Rethinking Agricultural and Rural Transformation in Africa – The Necessary Conditions for Success: The Case of Mauritius.* Addis Ababa: ECA.

ECA. (2017). *Africa Sustainable Development Report.* Addis Ababa: ECA.

Fox, L., Thomas, A., & Haines, C. (2017). *Structural Transformation in Employment and Productivity. What Can Africa Hope for?* Washington, DC: IMF.

IFPRI. (2013). *Global Hunger Index: The Challenge of Hunger: Building Resilience to Achieve Food and Nutrition Security.* Bonn, Washington, DC, Dublin: Welthungerhilfe, International Food Policy Research Institute and Concern Worldwide.

Lopes, C., Hamdock, A., & Elhiraika, A. (Eds.). (2017). *Macroeconomic Policy Framework for Africa's Structural Transformation.* London: Palgrave Macmillan.

McKinsey Global Institute. (2016). *Lions on the Move II*. London, New York: MGI.

Monga, C., & Lin, J. (Eds.). (2015). *The Oxford Handbook of Africa and Economics* (Vol. 2). Oxford: Oxford University Press.

NEPAD. (2010). *Accelerating CAADP Country Implementation*. Midrand: NEPAD.

NEPAD. (2013). *African Agriculture, Transformation and Outlook*. Midrand: NEPAD.

Rodrik, D. (2017). Growth Without Industrialization? *Project Syndicate*. Retrieved October 20, 2017, from https://www.project-syndicate.org/commentary/poor-economies-growing-without-industrializing-by-dani-rodrik-2017-10.

Severino, J.-M., & Hajdenberg, J. (2016). *Entreprenante Afrique*. Paris: Odile Jacob.

Timmer, C. P. (2005). *Agriculture and Pro-Poor Growth: An Asian Perspective*. Working Paper 63, Washington, DC: Center for Global Development.

Tsakok, I. (2011). *Success in Agricultural Transformation: What It Means and What Makes It Happen*. New York: Cambridge University Press.

von Grebmer, K., Saltzman, A., Birol, E., Wiesman, D., Prasai, N., Yin, S., et al. (2014). *Synopsis: 2014 Global Hunger Index: The Challenge of Hidden Hunger*. Washington, DC: IFPRI.

The World Bank. (2007). *World Bank Assistance to Agriculture in Sub-Saharan Africa: An IEG Review*. Washington, DC: World Bank.

The World Bank. (2010). *Building Competitiveness in African Agriculture*. Washington, DC: World Bank.

The World Bank. (2013). *Growing Africa: Unlocking the Potential of Agribusiness*. Washington, DC: World Bank.

Yumkella, K. K., Kormwa, P. M., Roerpstoff, T. M., & Hawkins, A. M. (2012). *Agribusiness for Africa's Prosperity*. Vienna: UNIDO.

CHAPTER 7

Revisiting the *Social Contract*

Rousseau emerges as the principal source of knowledge for nineteenth-century philosophy. It is rare that one man can epitomise such a wide range of attributes—democrat, romantic, educational theorist, botanist, composer, the man who stood for the underdog and the philosopher. In the 1760s, Rousseau's influence on education, sexuality, politics, and the self were brought into sharp focus in four of his most compelling literary pieces: *Social Contract*, *Emile*, *Julie*, and *The Confessions*.

The *Social Contract* emerges as Rousseau's most compelling and seminal piece of political theory. It explores legitimate political order in the context of classical republicanism. In his promulgation, 'man is born free but everywhere he is in chains', Rousseau asserts the inalienable rights of the individual and the sovereign 'will' of the people. According to Rousseau, freedom is natural, basic, and innate. Rousseau's idea of a form of social organisation that guarantees social autonomy, while still holding the values of a socially cohesive community sacred, is a recurrent theme in the *Social Contract*.

Rousseau's fundamental belief in collective law remains a timeless principle. In Rousseau's world, equity and freedom are essential ingredients for the establishment of a functional society. Rousseau's principle of collective governance is kindred in spirit to a multilateral policy system that advocates sustainable development as the principle of governance and institutional infrastructure. Today, 300 years after Rousseau's birth and 20 years after the original Rio Earth Summit and the following decades of

© The Author(s) 2019
C. Lopes, *Africa in Transformation*,
https://doi.org/10.1007/978-3-030-01291-5_7

multilateral negotiations, Rousseau's principles of social responsibility, civic freedom, and collective sovereignty are undergoing sharp scrutiny. In short, Rousseau's well-worn *Social Contract* has unmasked the complexity of reconfiguring the world's problems into a singular, dominant global governance regime.

What would Rousseau make of contemporary multilateralist surveillance regime, gridlocked in key areas that have direct links with human security? How would he come to terms with a society that seems to be at odds with the nature/society equilibrium that he staunchly advocated? Would Rousseau have been able to lift today's generation out of the collective myopia that focuses on individualism as the gateway to a prosperous future?

The rise of inequality across the world has revealed new governance challenges and made obvious the shortcomings of the state and market—two critical institutions—to act as regulatory forces. Can the principles found in Rousseau's *Social Contract* help in squaring this circle? Three centuries after Rousseau's compelling plea for social autonomy, multilateral institutions have not succeeded in mending the broken pieces of a social contract. Some of the questions that plagued Rousseau's world on inequality, freedom, poverty, nature, and society remain relevant even in contemporary society. Nation-states converge and diverge the subject of how to achieve the tenets of sustainable development in the same way that Rousseau's ideas divided public opinion of his time; rules remain the basis of social interactions.

I would like to propose a reinterpretation of Rousseau's principles posited in the *Social Contract* in light of a post-1992 Rio Earth Summit world.

If sustainable development is indeed considered as a global governance consensus, it would be important to understand what the Rio +20 Summit added to the older debate about the same principles. It will also be relevant to examine the perception of power asymmetries in today's multilateral regimes and governance.

We shall point to the fact that both Rousseau's principles and those of the two Rio Summits are essentially about change and that both argue for an institutional regime—a regime to uphold change through rules, social justice, and freedom. Institutions such as the 'Sovereign' State or an international regime (e.g. the United Nations) are perceived as necessary for charting the course of change. In essence states determine the contours as well as oversee and regulate its enforcement. Rousseau juxtaposes the natural versus the unnatural. He concedes that the maintenance of a social contract is contingent upon the process under which members of society determine the social order. This social order is not natural; it is created and maintained by humans in society. While acknowledging the role of social order, Rousseau is also alluding to the complex machinery, processes, and sustenance mechanisms that need to coexist along the vision of social order that he advocated. In today's more complex world, the arguments for a maintenance regime for sustainable development and a fairer society have become compelling.

I would like to argue that there are five conceptual arguments that can serve the reading of Rousseau's contribution to contemporary debates.

First, Rousseau's world of the *Social Contract* has several parallels with the post-1992 sustainable development world. As stated earlier, both Rousseau and the iconic Earth Summit are a part of change processes. In many ways, the entire concept of sustainable development can be interpreted as a process of change. However, it is an active process of regulation and self-regulation, adjustments and readjustments, with transmutations induced at all levels.

Second, Rousseau's social contract proposals cannot materialise without some form of association and an institutional architecture that will devise and uphold the 'rules of the game'. Equally, a sustainable development regime is maintained by an international structure, that is, a global system. Its enforcement and management will need robust institutions for the monitoring of progress.

> 'The problem is to find a form of association which will defend and protect with the whole common force the person and goods of each associate, and in which each, while uniting himself with all, may still obey himself alone, and remain as free as before'. This is the fundamental problem of which the social contract provides the solution.

Rousseau's essential yardstick for success resides in the way institutions are sought as the means to maintain social order and cohesion. Rousseau's state of law comes to full representation in an environment of economic institutions. A social contract is born out of this institutional glue. The existence of rule of law represents the existence of institutions that are governed by rules that determine the way each individual in society deals with others (North 1990). Rousseau's social contract is strongly equated with good institutions, and it can be sustained only if the individuals within the system do not attempt to dislodge it. In Rousseau's view, the state of nature is the natural default action for humankind; yet, the danger is that when the state of nature is in place, resources tend to be wasted in expropriation and rent-seeking activities (Cervellati 2005).

Third, Rousseau's narrative of freedom has the same motivations as the notion of sustainable development and the principles embodied in Agenda 21. Agenda 21, the blueprint adopted by the United Nations for how countries can achieve sustainable development, gives voice and agency to all stakeholders that is way beyond the traditional role played by governments. It puts participation at the centre of the debate and presents local actors as the frontrunners in deciding how strategies can be formulated and actions can be implemented. Rousseau's freedom narrative may sound ambiguous and even contradictory. Rousseau posed the challenge as follows:

> Find a form of association which defends and protects with all common forces the person and goods of each associate, and by means of which each one, while uniting with all, nevertheless obeys only himself and remains as free as before. (In Book I of the *Social Contract*, Chap. VI)

The question remains, why must the move to a political society leave everyone as free as before? How does one reconcile the freedom a government has to use coercion, in order to make its citizenry obey its will, with the freedom of the coerced citizens? It should be clear that the principles of sustainable development cannot be understood in the absence of real freedom.

Sen's idea of expanding the concept of development to include freedom, understood as access to basic entitlements, is linked to the tenets of sustainability and the Rousseauian ideal. According to Sen, deprivation is strongly associated with the absence of entitlement to some good rather than the absence of the good itself (Sen 2009). He argues that in the context of a famine, the default analysis is not an absolute absence of food or poverty but rather the absence of entitlement to the food that is available. Sen asserts that famine tends to not occur in a country where free press and openness are observed. In short when victims of famine make their plight visible governments are compelled to respond. To a larger extent Sen poses a fundamental question to Rawls, and other political theorists such as Rousseau: if justice is reduced to the product of a contract, who will uphold the interest of non-contractors, foreigners to the contract, and future generations? These interested parties might be overlooked by the observance of such a contract.

The Rousseauian idea of the 'general will' is a metaphor for social autonomy. It is indicative of the sustainability of societies, acting collectively to ensure that future generations do not have to bear the burden and correct the wrongs of the present generations. The notion of intergenerational equity mirrors Rousseau's 'general will' as a symbol of law that will work for the collective good of citizens. Our collective force in a Rousseauian world can be exercised when our dependence is depersonalised, and we embrace the community as a way of escaping social ills. The 'general will' becomes the principal role of reconfiguring forms of dependence. It ensures that society is properly structured to uphold the freedoms for each individual. The 'General', Rousseau's short hand for the state, will also establish the rule of law to ensure that all members of society are equally treated. Rousseau's sense of 'enlightened self-interest', in which individual members of society become recognised by propping up each other's self-esteem, is the same vision as that forwarded by Agenda 21—a vision that reinforces the principle that by acting today in harnessing the earth's resources, one is merely acting in one's and the future generations' interests.

Fourth, the notion of power also allows a comparator of Rousseau's 'General' to the dominant state and the multiplicity of non-state actors in today's complex world. The management of global problems goes beyond the responsibility and purview of the unitary state actor. This is a very different reality from that of Rousseau's world, where the state was 'omnipresent'. The implications of managing global issues, such as climate change, trade, or transboundary resources, are not respectful of borders. They tend to 'leak' and 'spill' over national boundaries (Castree 2003: 423e–439).

The state may exercise its legitimacy and authority within national boundaries, but non-state actors in the form of international regimes continue to assert their authority and governance models, with many countries facing the same global challenges. Today's dominant state, with the principle of sovereignty as its protagonist, is losing ground. International regimes are in high demand for the expansion of collective territoriality of the state and reduction of the transaction costs. They act as providers of information and facilitators of interstate cooperation (Hasenclever et al. 1997).

With international regimes wielding greater authority in the regulation of global governance processes, the role of the state has been weakened. Rousseau's social contract does not reflect the proliferation of
non-state actors in an increasingly complex world. Global challenges,
such as biodiversity, climate change, and international trade, remain state
prerogatives. Boundaries confer both sovereignty and exclusivity to the
state. When some state powers are shared or ceded to international
regimes as part of a process, it is done with a prerogative to roll back any
decision that is contrary to the interests of the sovereignty. As Paterson
argues, the

> fundamental (yet largely unacknowledged, and certainly unexamined) com-
> mitments in this understanding of global environmental politics are of an
> inter-state understanding of global politics, a liberal understanding of politi-
> cal economy, and of the neutrality of science. (Paterson 2001: 32)

A *fifth* parallel between Rousseau and the post-1992 world can be found
in the immediacy of institutions as emblematic structures for change. It is
worth noting that Sen offers a counterargument to Rawls, and even
Rousseau, on the importance of institutions as upholders of the rule of
law. Rousseau's social contract is intimately linked to an institutional order
as the main legislator of rules that predetermines social behaviour. The
naïve assumption is that the right set of institutions will prevail. Little
importance is given to contradictory human behaviour. As Kant put it,
even a race of devils, if intelligent, could produce just institutions and a
just society. The current international governance and decision-making
processes unmask this assertion.

Sen's depiction of Sanskrit literature on ethics and jurisprudence out-
lines the difference between *Niti* and *Nyaya*. A careful analysis of both
terms reveals their association with justice, but they both summarise different notions. *Niti* refers to correct procedures, institutions, and formal
rules, whereas *Nyaya* is a more all-encompassing term that looks to the
world that emerges from the institutions we create, rather than merely
mirroring the structures of institutions. Hence, Sen, similar to points
made by Adam Smith, North, and Mills, about the importance of having
a more holistic representation of institutions, looks at them not just
through the prism of realisation, but, more inclusively, considering other
factors, such as human behaviour.

UNDERSTANDING CURRENT SUSTAINABLE DEVELOPMENT GOVERNANCE MODEL

When in 2002, activists, policymakers, and stakeholders met in Rio de Janeiro again under the auspices of the United Nations (20 years after the first Earth Summit), the common intent was to chart a course for the future of humanity. This 'new' resolve was reminiscent of the commitments that global leaders rehearsed before, pledging them to lift people out of poverty and protect the earth. The Rio +20 Summit was intended as a celebration of the original Summit of 1992. Beyond a celebration of past commitments, Rio +20 was also meant to reaffirm political commitments and help global leaders take concrete actions to move towards a green economy. Further, 20 years later, the world had become a more complex place where poverty and inequality remained staple attributes. So, what is the verdict? Well, many pundits describe Rio +20 as a 'nonevent', a 'failure in leadership', a 'vague agreement', or a 'weak outcome'.

Scientists and activists alike had pinned their hopes on a conference that would emphasise the expediency of a world in distress. But, it is not just earth's life system that is under threat; it is the population of more than one billion people who go to bed hungry every night that one needs to be addressed. This stark reality is certainly an aggravation of what Rousseau observed in the eighteenth century, at least in size and complexity. Rio +20 may appear as a demonstration of how the world is getting worse rather than better.

Critics of Rio +20 seem to have forgotten the controversy of the 1992 Earth Summit. It was perceived by some critics as having failed to set a new direction for life on earth. When one attempts to fast-forward 20 years, one can quickly discern the remarkable positive evaluation the conference has received since.

No matter the complexion of the immediate evaluation of the 2012 United Nations World Summit on Sustainable Development, it is, nevertheless, clear that the countries failed to design their cooperation mechanisms in ways that can provide a new momentum for the implementation of Agenda 21. The summit simply laid bare the fact that global commitments—with their strict targets and uniform measurements of progress—were politically unrealistic (Papa and Gleason 2012). Therein lay both the challenge and the paradox.

Further, 300 years after the birth of Rousseau and the foundation of social autonomy, can global leaders come up with a 'blueprint' to regulate the affairs of so many diverse people, economies, ecosystems, and social formations? How can this uniformity in measurement enable and kick-start action on key principles associated with the social contract, that is, equity, freedom, the rule of law, and the like?

Yet, kick-starting some of the principles of sustainable development has further polarised the world in the 2012 Rio; global leaders have channelled their energies to define what green economy is and what it is not. The term achieved diplomatic momentum at the summit. Many developing countries were concerned that this new concept will replace sustainable development. Advocates of sticking only to sustainable development felt that major policy matters on finance and technology were deliberately forgotten in the interest of an even looser term. Hence, the debate was given an ideological and semantic resonance.

Some countries, mostly from the South, asserted that the green economy is simply a component of sustainable development and should not be used to dictate the pace of international policy governance. For richer countries, greening the economy (through clean energy) could be a safe pathway to increasing economic growth and creating new 'green' jobs. Subsequently, the efforts to adopt a green economy road map with environmental targets, goals, and deadlines met with great resistance in Rio.

Rio produced the typical asymmetrical relationships with the EU, on one hand, insisting on emphasis upon energy, water resource efficiency, and land and ecosystems as critical areas for measuring Sustainable Development Goals (SDGs); whilst Group of 77 plus China, on the other hand, placed more emphasis upon greater balance between the three pillars of sustainable development (economic, social, and environmental). Another problem evident in the outcomes of the summit was concerned with the controversy around the issues of finance and technology and the means of implementation. The cleavage between the developed and developing countries on this topic is even deeper. Developing countries argue that leapfrogging environmentally sound technologies should mean that structured support from industrialised nations can be gleaned. This was a key plank of the argument of developing countries in 1992, and it remained a constant one in the negotiations 20 years later. The question of new and additional financial flows and respect for the agreed aid target of 0.7% of industrialised countries' GDP was avoided systematically.

IS SUSTAINABLE DEVELOPMENT AN IMPRACTICAL CONCEPT FOR GLOBAL GOVERNANCE?

Sustainable development was born out of a historical context. The theory was an attempt to resolve the tension between environmental concerns resulting from the ecological consequences of human activities on one hand and economic, social, and political concerns on the other. The central tenet of sustainable development resides in the concept of equity and social justice for all. This is often associated with Rawlsian theory that suggests a bias in resource allocation to benefit the least-advantaged societies (Rawls 1971). The intergenerational solidarity principle translated into the will, which states that resource management of today should not compromise the wellbeing of the future generations, remains popular till date.

More than two decades after the concept was given visibility by the Brundtland Report, our understanding of sustainable development is still evolving (Newman 2006: 633–637). Indeed, subsequent international conferences, such as the World Summit on Sustainable Development held in Johannesburg in 2002, reinforced the need for change in the way societies produce and consume as a precondition for achieving sustainable development (ECA 2009). In fact, the ECA's 'Sustainable Development Report' emphasises the importance of moving towards sustainable consumption and production to fulfil the dual aspirations of economic growth and poverty alleviation.

The term 'sustainable development' also implies balance, that is, the ability to use the different capitals (social, natural, physical) in ways that do not jeopardise natural support systems (Kates 2001). The amount and distribution of the various capitals matter (Kates and Dasgupta 2007). The terminology has achieved greater political legitimacy as argued by the Brundtland Commission. The environment is where we live, and development is what we all do while attempting to improve our lot within that abode. The two are inseparable.

Yet, in spite of this evolution, sustainable development continues to suffer from definitional vagueness (Happaerts 2012: 2–17). Most critics of sustainable development tend to see it as being far too normative and ambiguous and as being incapable of bringing practical solutions to complex development and environmental problems (Newman 2006). To break away from this inherent fuzziness and ambiguity, the term 'sustainability' is invariably used as a substitute for the absence of clarity in the path towards development. As Holling (1973: 1–23) argues, 'sustainability is the capacity to 'create, test and maintain adaptive capability'. Development, on the other hand, can be a process of environmental management that is evolutionary in nature.

The new so-called engines of global growth, such as Brazil, Russia, India, and China, have a collective GDP that is getting closer to that of Japan, France, the United Kingdom, Italy, Germany, and the United States put together (Nayyar 2010). Yet, in spite of their colossal economies and growth trajectories, their roles in acting as models or champions for sustainable development have been overlooked. What is their potential for achieving sustainable development? China is an example of a country that has achieved growth but has not necessarily linked growth to the principles of environmental preservation.

Critics argue that the sustainable development concept needs to be more flexible and dynamic, that it should be able to lend itself to ecological and social realities. Sustainable development is a process of transformative change across scales and governance regimes. Sustainable development requires an enabling environment, robust institutions, and a set of rules to be adhered to. These are not processes that one can 'stumble' upon. These will require continuous direction and focus.

ASYMMETRIES IN THE CURRENT MULTILATERAL REGIMES AND GOVERNANCE

The challenge of a multilateral governance model that advocates sustainable development cannot be severed from a model that is able to set global agendas, legitimises principles of common actions, and brings global communities to commit to a process of implementing change at the local, national, and international levels. This operational space can happen only in an architecture with actors that fully accept multilateral diplomacy, with the United Nations providing the critical platform for multiparty negotiations.

Principles such as 'common but differentiated responsibility', 'subsidiarity', and the 'the polluter pays' have become synonymous with an institutional structure that is largely perceived as an enforcer. As in Rousseau's social contract, the seeds for a transformative development are deeply rooted in the capacity of the perceived institution and how it induces change.

The asymmetries of the world, hitherto anchored mainly in the North/South divide, have become even more diffused and stratified with wide-ranging inequalities that can be found in technology, science, and even the basic production system. Thus, the expectation that the North will provide the key to unlocking development in the South is a 'pipe' dream. Many of the big OECD countries have channelled their energies elsewhere and concerns on how efficient and clean technologies can be transferred have remained mere rhetorical questions (Goldin 2016).

Global leaders such as the EU have not succeeded in persuading a disinterested United States to take a stronger role in the management of global commons (Goldin 2016; Vogler and Hannes 2007). Consequently, the paradox is that the role of the United Nations in managing the state of equilibrium between the three pillars of sustainable development has become more difficult. The South-prevailing viewpoint focuses on environmental degradation as the chief culprit for their growing problems of poverty and deprivation. The voices of the Group of 77 plus China seem to become even more discordant than before. Yet, we are in a world where coalition politics and key networks increase their bargaining power.

How can Rousseau's social contract principle be given more relevance in a complex world, where present generations are held accountable by future generations? Justice between generations is becoming even more compelling. With growing environmental degradation and economic stagnation, the idea of justice between generations was felt acutely in the 1970s. Indeed, the welfare of future generations has resonated throughout the generations as a predominant ideology, often expressed in 'faith in the future'. The Renaissance, or 'rebirth' from sleep, and the eighteenth-century Enlightenment period all promoted the idea of progress in human affairs. In the nineteenth-century world, this continued interest in human progress was associated with the Industrial Revolution. However, by the twentieth century, the future was mired in pessimism—what with World War II, the Holocaust, and the spectre of a nuclear war.

Whatever the strength of this 'master narrative', the notion of intergenerational equity and solidarity shapes the global governance regimes. One could argue that previous political theorists have not sufficiently thought through the notion of reciprocity. Indeed, the utilitarian principle based on the 'greatest good for the greatest number' seemingly placed more emphasis upon the quantity of life rather than the quality and upon how this will put future generations at risk. Rousseau, Kant, and Locke present a challenge to the notion of reciprocity. In short, if our current actions have implications for future generations, how can our lives be affected by unborn generations?

Obligations to future generations present a central ethical problem, in terms of both how to approach the reality of an ageing population in most of the developing countries, in significant part of Asia and Latin America, and a booming younger population in Africa. Let us consider this conundrum. In the interest of intergenerational equity, how can we draw up a new social contract that will consider changing demographic dynamics?

The answer to this 'riddle' will lie in the ability to right the youth asymmetry that the world is currently witnessing. In its latest report on the global population trends, the United Nations said that the world's population will increase to 7.2 billion and is projected to reach 10.9 billion by 2100. Population growth is likely to increase in the world's poorest countries with high fertility rates, which are mainly concentrated in Africa. It is estimated that half of population growth between 2013 and 2100 will be concentrated in just eight countries, which are as follows: the Democratic Republic of Congo, Ethiopia, Niger, Nigeria, India, Tanzania, Uganda, and the United States.

The current youth dynamics in Africa present a challenge. It is reported that in less than three generations, 41% of the world youth will be Africans. It is believed that between 2010 and 2020, Africa will add an additional 163 million people to its potential labour force. In addition, the African labour force is set to increase and outgrow that of China by 2035. Approximately 54% of Africa's youth is currently unemployed and more than three-quarters live on less than US $2 a day. In Africa, there is a tendency for youth unemployment to increase with the increase in education levels. Another constant factor is that government programmes, aimed at promoting youth employment, tend to be inefficient. This is the case for at least 21 countries in Africa.

This generation of young people have an enormous potential to expand Africa's productive workforce, promote job creation and entrepreneurship, and harness the enormous resources that the continent is endowed with. Poor investment in today's and tomorrow's youth can constitute a blessing or a curse for the continent. Balancing the development sheet need to be done in ways that do not leave the majority of the world's population disenfranchised.

But how prepared is Africa to deflect the potential tension that can arise from an urban youth population that is rapidly growing, educated, unemployed, frustrated, and lacks a political space? Given the relative stagnation of employment in the 15–24 age bracket, how can Africa design and use a new social contract to ensure that the marginalised youth is not written off and fully absorbed in the economy?

The real challenge of the twenty-first century will lie in developing the ability to address this demographic mega trend in a manner that will preserve the interests of future generations. How can a new social contract realign the disenfranchised, the old, the young, and the poor back to the centre of a development agenda? Today's elderly generation in Europe or Japan is able to enjoy a relatively prosperous old age, mainly because their working lives are comparatively more prosperous than those of their parents. To what extent can Europe or Japan sustain its social welfare system without renegotiating a new contract with Africa's youth?

Rewriting a new social contract implicitly means that there is a level of dissatisfaction with the way our world is configured. How do we create a redistributive system that is 'solidarity-like' and helps to enhance both intra-generational and intergenerational equity? How do we create new institutions that can lift people out of poverty based on a social contract that seeks to provide security and welfare to the poorest in the remotest outposts of the world?

The Rio rationale, from 20 years ago, is not radically dissimilar to the Rousseauian ideal of freedom and justice and the need for a participatory form of democracy that becomes the model of choice. A wholesale shift from the Rousseauian ideal to a new contract that will consider intergenerational equity will ensure that institutions aligned to societal needs will be hard to develop. However, there are real risks for policymakers and humankind in general if we dismiss these ideals by deeming them as being merely utopian. The collective interest is strongly rooted in the ability to institute the behavioural response that will ensure that, whilst cognisant of a risk-sharing approach, opportunities are provided to future generations.

The unanimous adoption of a new universal Agenda 2030 by the United Nations followed by the new climate deal resulting from the Paris' United Nations Climate Change Conference of the Parties, both in 2015, created an expectation that a breathing space had been established. Yet one year later, the rolling back of multilateralism is the focus of the debates on global governance. Africa participated in the definition of the new agenda with a rare sense of urgency, a demonstration of unity and emphatic agency. It therefore feels even more frustrated, given that this 'show of multilateralism' was, this time around, in favour of the continent's self-identified priorities.

The recent political developments have demonstrated that the principles that framed the understanding of intergenerational solidarity can and are being questioned when it is sociologically perceived that migrants from other regions are taking jobs from the citizens of Western countries. Upon listening carefully to the populist arguments against opening societies that espouse multilateralism and expand humanitarianism, it becomes clear that the discussion about demographic megatrends is unnerving. In the very near future, exercising intergenerational solidarity will entail a need for ageing countries to embrace those with a very young population. The latter are mostly African and the former mostly Western. This is indeed a new brave world that many are not ready for.

REFERENCES

Castree, N. (2003). The Geopolitics of Nature. In J. Agnew, K. Mitchell, & G. Toal (Eds.), *A Companion to Political Geography* (pp. 423–439). Oxford: Blackwell.

Cervellati, M. (2005). *Hobbes to Rousseau: Inequality, Institutions and Development.* Issue 1450 of Discussion Paper, IZA.

ECA. (2009). *African Governance Report II.* Oxford: Oxford University Press.

Goldin, I. (Ed.). (2016). *Is the Planet Full?* Oxford: Oxford University Press.

Happaerts, S. (2012). Sustainable Development and Subnational Governments: Going beyond Symbolic Politics? *Environmental Development, 4,* 2–17.

Hasenclever, A., Mayer, P., & Rittberger, V. (1997). *Theories of International Regimes.* Cambridge: Cambridge University Press.

Holling, C. S. (1973). Resilience and Stability of Ecological Systems. *Annual Review of Ecology and Systematics, 4,* 1–23.

Kates, R. W. (2001). Sustainability Science. *Science, 292*(5517), 641–642.

Kates, R. W., & Dasgupta, P. (2007). African Poverty: A Grand Challenge for Sustainability Science. *Proceedings of the National Academy of Sciences, 104*(43), 16747–16750.

Nayyar, D. (2010). *Trade and Globalization.* Mumbai: Oxford University Press.

Newman, L. (2006). Change, Uncertainty, and Futures of Sustainable Development. *Futures, 38*(5), 633–637.

North, D. (1990). *Institutions, Institutional Change and Economic Performance, Political Economy of Institutions and Decisions.* St. Louis: Washington University.

Papa, M., & Gleason, N. (2012). Major Emerging Powers in Sustainable Development. *Global Environmental Change, 22*(4), 915–924.

Paterson, M. (2001). *Understanding Global Environmental Politics: Domination, Accumulation, Resistance.* Basingstoke: Palgrave Macmillan.

Rawls, J. A. (1971). *Theory of Justice.* Cambridge, MA: Belknap Press.

Rousseau, J. J. (1761). *Julie.*

Rousseau, J. J. (1762a). *Emile.*

Rousseau, J. J. (1762b). *The Social Contract and Discourses.*

Rousseau, J. J. (1789). *The Confessions 1782–1789.*

Sen, A. (2009). *The Idea of Justice.* Cambridge: Harvard University Press.

Vogler, J., & Hannes, S. (2007). The European Union in Global Environmental Governance: Leadership in the Making? *International Environmental Agreements: Politics, Law and Economics, 7*(4), 389–413.

CHAPTER 8

Adjusting to Climate Change

If we go back in history, we all remember the time when the Black Death plague killed so many people that people at that time must have thought it was the end of their world. Important civilisations died without clear explanations for their sudden removal from the face of Earth. The Black Death was particularly acute in Europe, spreading poverty and decimating livelihoods. What came next though was a spectacular transformation, because less people had more resources. As a result, agriculture flourished and trade spread. With the Industrial Revolution came urbanisation, better modes of improved communication, and a deep change in the social fabric. For over 100 years, the United Kingdom led the Industrial Revolution, and cotton and cotton-derived products were the number one export item.

These historical episodes are all related to climate change. It was climate change variations that were at the root of the Black Death. It was the stability of climate that ensued, and lasted for 300 years, that made allowance for unprecedented human progress witnessed in the wealthiest regions of the world. Predictable winds propelled global routes. Access to water and other key resources was abundant and remained so for a long time.

Well that time is now over, and we know it. We all now certainly need the opportunity and space to discuss key issues deriving from striking findings and an unpredictable future. In my opinion, we need to particularly bear in mind two interrelated issues.

© The Author(s) 2019
C. Lopes, *Africa in Transformation*,
https://doi.org/10.1007/978-3-030-01291-5_8

First, there is a need to persuade the sceptics of climate change in Africa on the urgency of just how vulnerable we are to it. We should do this by navigating scientific findings and hard facts that make its impact unequivocal. According to the recently released report of the Intergovernmental Panel on Climate Change (IPCC), the last three decades have been successively warmer than observed in any other preceding decade since the 1850s. In the Northern Hemisphere, 1983–2012 was most likely the warmest 30-year period observed in the last 1400 years. Scientists further predict that the current pace of warming is ten times faster than that observed in any other time in the last 65 million years.

REPOSITIONING THE DEBATE

Warming across Africa is predicted to rise at an alarming rate. Some of the effects of climate variability across the continent are obvious. For instance, the severe droughts of 2011 in the Horn of Africa and the 2012 drought in the Sahel region affected over 23 million people. There is also the example of ongoing coastal erosion and the rising sea levels that threaten the very existence of Africa's Small Island Developing States. Floods devastated Port-Louis, Mauritius' beautiful capital, in 2015. They were caused by 156 mm of rainfall that occurred in just less than two hours, resulting in major damage. The impact of rising seas and increasingly violent and frequent storms can make many tourist beaches disappear by 2050. Even Africa's grand continental symbol, the Kilimanjaro, is fast losing its white cap.

Africa continues to be patronised and perceived as a victim of climate change as opposed to a contributor to the solution. It is as if the debate on climate was reduced to how Africa can adapt to what others cause, indirectly questioning whether it is time to industrialise and follow others' successful path (ECA 2016a). This is wrong and this needs to be counterargued.

The type of industrialisation path Africa chooses will make a significant difference. Africa possesses some of the best resource base for commodity-based industrial production. Exporting the resources far away deprives Africans of jobs and the world of sustainability, given that the CO_2 emissions impact current flows. Africa exports jobs, precisely when it is about to become the largest reservoir of manpower, and the rate at which this is done is projected to surpass that of China or India by 2040. Shifting production closer to the source would be economically beneficial for Africa as this move will create sustainable employment and generate wealth. There will also be something in it for producers, given the increasing industrial unit value accrual in Asia. If it took the United Kingdom 155 years to double its GDP in any time in its history, and Africa has achieved the same in the last 12, it is imperative to capitalise on such a performance.

As countries grow, they become cleaner, more urban, more peaceful, more efficient, and better informed. As already mentioned this rationale is based on some sort of environmental version of the famous Kuznets' curve, which sketches the relationship between prosperity and inequality in an inverted U shape (Kuznets 1955). In a nutshell, at the initial stages of growth, inequality tends to rise; at the later stages, it falls. Similarly, in the initial stages of growth, biodiversity tends to suffer; in the later stages, it benefits. We can see this relationship taking form in countries like Brazil and South Korea that were considered poor until recently.

As one of the most vulnerable continents to climate change, Africa's growth momentum faces a fundamental risk. For instance, agricultural production and food security could be severely compromised, given that more than 90% of Africa's agricultural production is rain-fed, and, therefore, highly vulnerable to the impacts of climate change. It is estimated that by 2020, yields from rain-fed agriculture in some African countries could decrease by as much as 50%, exacerbating the food security challenges. Needless to say: this would bring about dire socio-economic consequences upon the livelihoods of farmers, pastoralists, and agro-pastoralists. The situation could be further compounded by acute water stress in some countries as well as intense changes, occurring across a variety of ecosystems (AfDB et al. 2013).

Rapid urbanisation and a population that is projected to double in size (to eventually amount to 2.3 billion people over the next 40 years, comprising about half of the globe's total population growth) offer a daunting picture. It could trigger competition for the available resources. It can expose the world to a breaking point, with the largest and fastest urbanisation seen in history. It can wield devastating effects on a unique biodiversity (Goldin 2016; Kelly 2016; AfDB et al. 2015).

I have been advocating that climate change can be used as a golden opportunity for green industrialisation. Industrialising on a business-as-usual approach makes little sense for Africa and the costs of such a path would be unacceptably high. The continent needs to adopt a low-carbon and inclusive pathway, by using finite resources efficiently, reducing the harm to the environment, while increasing the global competitiveness of its enterprises because they are anchored on long-term business sustainability.

This is a model that requires a step-wise change, recognising that changes at the margins will not suffice (ECA 2016b; Brahmbhatt et al. 2017). There is a need for a growth pattern that will give agency and confidence to communities that have long stood at the periphery of development. Obviously, this is not going to happen spontaneously. It needs coherent policies entrenched in a coherent development strategy, with bold measures. I have suggested before that it can happen through key actions (ECA 2016b) such as: (1) a review of national development plans and strategies to identify opportunities and entry points for green industrialisation, and thus develop an economy-wide green-growth vision; (2) identification of clear, consistent, and coherent policies and interventions, involving all key stakeholders; (3) building partnerships and leveraging limited public resources to mobilise investments from the private sector and various sources aligned with national priorities; (4) investing in innovation, infrastructure, collaborative research, regional integration, and trade as key enablers; and (5) adoption of a learning-by-doing approach with space for corrections and adjustments.

Growth that protects Africa's natural environment, and the earth's global commons, is a must for the region that is the worst affected by climate. In practice, that means more efficient use of water and energy, the adoption of cleaner technologies, and governments promoting innovation and risk-taking by entrepreneurs. Many lead small, gazelle-like businesses that are dynamic and quick, with high productivity and potential for rapid growth. Entrepreneurs can thrive in small-scale clean energy industries, such as household solar, clean stoves, waste management, and sanitation (Brahmbhatt et al. 2017).

Green industrialisation and thriving entrepreneurship can propel Africa's leap into a transformative path. If the continent collectively orchestrates this effort, global conditions are ripe for this transformation to take hold. Green technology is progressing, and its costs are falling every day. Global green markets are growing at a breath-taking pace, trading everything from wind turbines to organic fertilisers. In 2016, the world invested US $241.6 billion in renewable energy, double the amount in fossil fuel investment. 'Industries without smokestacks', such as ecotourism and remote IT support, are burgeoning—bringing the economic advantages of manufacturing without the environmental costs (Brahmbhatt et al. 2017).

Africa has vast clean energy resources that can take a lead in the global renewable energy market (ECA 2016b). It has some of the best biomass, geothermal, hydropower, wind, and solar resources in the world and we have only just scratched the surface of our full potential. The already unprecedented pace of innovation is evidenced by a rapid growth of pay-as-you-go solar home systems linked to mobile payment technology. More than 450,000 such systems have been deployed in east Africa alone, and some 60 million Africans may already be using off-grid renewable electricity of some kind. This is not a futuristic vision, but a description of a future that is already happening (Brahmbhatt et al. 2017).

Many policy directives and incentives are needed to foster this transformation. Amongst them are: adopting green urban policies to promote compact, connected, and coordinated cities; strengthening 'export push' policies, including support for green exports by identifying markets and improving certification and standards; and investing in sustainable infrastructure and increased infrastructure efficiency.

THE SPECIAL IMPORTANCE OF THE BLUE ECONOMY

The richness of Africa is particularly significant if its 'blue economy', made of vast lakes and rivers and an extensive ocean resource base, is accounted for. Thirty-eight out of the 44 African states are coastal. More than 90% of Africa's imports and exports are conducted by sea, and some of the most strategic gateways for international trade are in Africa, underscoring the geopolitical importance of the region. Maritime zones under Africa's jurisdiction cover about 13 million square kilometres, including territorial seas, and approximately 6.5 million square kilometres of the continental shelf. Mauritius, with its 1850 square kilometres, is one of the smallest countries in Africa and in the world. However, with its territorial waters, it becomes a country with 1.9 million square kilometres, the size of South Africa (ECA 2016c). Therefore, we have another Africa under the sea. Quite rightly, the AU calls the blue economy the 'New Frontier of African Renaissance'.

Africa's aquatic and marine spaces are an increasingly common topic of political discourse; its natural resources have remained largely underexploited but are now being recognised for their potential contribution to inclusive and sustainable development. This 'blue economy' is more than just an economic space—it is part of Africa's rich geographical, social, and cultural canvas. Through a better understanding of the enormous opportunities, emerging from investing and reinvesting in Africa's aquatic and marine spaces, the balance can be tipped away from illegal harvesting, degradation, and depletion to a sustainable blue development paradigm, serving Africa today and tomorrow. If fully exploited and well managed, Africa's blue economy can constitute a major source of wealth and catapult the continent's fortunes (FAO 2014).

Africa's economies continue to grow at remarkable rates through the exploitation of the rich endowment of land-based natural resources and commodity exports. Converting this growth into quality growth, through the generation of inclusive wealth within environmental limits and in observance of the highest social considerations, requires bold new thinking (Costanza et al. 2009). It also involves the creation of jobs for a population on the rise. The blue economy offers that opportunity. For example, the International Energy Agency estimates that the ocean renewable energy has power potential that is sufficient to provide up to 400% of the current global energy demand. Other estimates indicate that in 2010, the total annual economic value of maritime-related activities reached €1.5 trillion. It is forecasted that by 2020, this figure will reach €2.5 trillion per year. Surely, Africa needs holistic and coherent strategies to harness this potential.

All water bodies, including lakes, rivers, and underground water, in addition to seas and the coast, are all unique resources; yet they are neglected, and often forgotten. The largest sectors of the current African aquatic and ocean-based economy are fisheries, aquaculture, tourism, transport, ports, coastal mining, and energy. Additionally, the blue economy approach emphasises interconnectedness with other sectors, is responsive to the emerging and frontier sectors, and supports important social considerations, such as gender mainstreaming, food and water security, poverty alleviation, wealth retention, and job creation. Thus, the blue economy can play a significant role in Africa's structural transformation.

The approach advocated here is premised in the sustainable use, management, and conservation of aquatic and marine ecosystems and associated resources. It builds on principles of equity, low-carbon footprint, resource efficiency, social inclusion, and broad-based development, with the jobs agenda at the centre of it all. It is anchored in strong regional cooperation and integration, considers structural transformation as an imperative for Africa's development, and advocates for a complete departure from the enclave development models. Instead, through better linkages to other sectors of the economy, it situates the aquatic and marine economies as being a part of the integrated ecosystem services based on the harvesting of living and non-living resources, benefitting both costal, island states and landlocked countries.

Biotic resources allow Africa to expand its fishing, aquaculture, and agriculture sectors, and it fosters the emergence of vibrant pharmaceutical, chemical, and cosmetics industries. The extraction of mineral resources and the generation of new energy resources provide the feedstock to resource-based industrialisation and places Africa, being at the centre of the global trade in value-added products, as no longer being a supplier of unprocessed raw materials. Central to this agenda is the need to modernise Africa's maritime transport and logistics services, its port, and railway infrastructure as well as improve its reliability and efficiency with the view to seamlessly link the continent's economies to national, regional, and global value chains along with facilitating tourism and recreation activities, just to cite a few pressing requirements (ECA 2016c).

Africa has shown salutary examples of maritime, riparian, and river-based cooperation and dispute settlement. This includes examples of maritime and transnational aquatic boundary delimitation and demarcation. A collaborative approach for the development of the blue economy will create the foundation for the formulation of shared visions for transformation. The blue economy development approach is an integral part of the AU's Agenda 2063. Building on the experience of implementing green economy principles for a transition to low-carbon development, we are seeing an increasing number of African member states formulating blue economy strategies to diversify their economic base and catalyse socio-economic transformation.

How to Better Negotiate?

To make an impact on transformation environmental concerns, be it for green industrialisation or catapulting the blue economy, it is fundamental to operate in two fronts. At the level of policy introduce clarity, sophistication, and sense of urgency. But Africa is not alone in the world. The effects of climate change are observed throughout the continent. The negative impact is already felt and the loss of biodiversity, livelihoods, and economic potential palpable.

Africa is trapped in global negotiations on climate change, which, on the whole, are largely driven by global and external interests. To enter the solution space, Africa must embolden its own views on how to put the continent's interest first. Climate change offers Africa an array of incredible investment opportunities that can reap dividends. Offering an African climate development policy can respond to the unique vulnerabilities and opportunities the continent faces, while positioning it to influence negotiations and outcomes.

As mentioned earlier in the previous chapter, Africa has the potential to enter into a new clean techno-economic paradigm. For instance, the European Commission's Institute for Energy suggests that just 0.3% of the sunlight that shines on the Sahara and the Middle East deserts could supply all of Europe's energy needs. As Africa is not locked in any technology preferences, it can follow a green and clean energy pathway, leapfrog old carbon-intensive models, and pursue a low-carbon development pathway. The growing awareness of environmental degradation and climate change is giving rise to new research and design priorities such as clean energy technologies that could be scaled up rapidly. The continent is well positioned to absorb, adapt, and build on the vast quantities of scientific and technical knowledge that is already available. Many African countries, such as Cabo Verde, Kenya, Ethiopia, Morocco, or Uganda, are already investing in innovative renewable and clean energy sectors and offsetting traditional energy sources dependent on fossil fuels, biomass, and forest resources.

It is obvious that greater investment in climate science, services, and the production of high-quality data is imperative for Africa. This is to facilitate the development of early warning systems and initiate the much-needed research on climate impact, vulnerability, and adaptation as well as for the creation of a knowledge economy. Many global, African, and national institutions are already making progress in transforming climate data, information systems, and science. Thus, the stage is set for Africa to enter the path of sustainable development.

Several institutions are promoting a discussion on African climate research frontiers in order to guide research that will contribute to climate information and knowledge, inform policy decisions, and promote development planning. In order to reinforce such successful networks, Africa needs to improve its institutional and policy capacity. There must be investment in mechanisms for a concerted engagement of climate and social scientists, development economists, policymakers, entrepreneurs, and users of climate information. Not only would this help coordinate efforts, it would also contribute to the design of innovative multisectoral strategies but also result in the mainstreaming of climate change into national development plans as well as usher in a new form of deliberative democracy. To prepare for climate risks in urban infrastructure, countries could build climate-proof infrastructure and put transport systems on a low-carbon path, like what has been done in Côte d'Ivoire, Algeria, Ethiopia, South Africa, and others.

With a growing population and an ever-increasing demand for food, investments in agriculture are critical. Investing in production technologies, innovation, water use efficiency, and sustainable land management is essential. As pointed above, the bulk of agricultural export across the continent is still predominantly in the form of primary products, with very limited value-addition. Leveraging the capacity of the private sector to scale up investment in agro-processing would create jobs and diversify export commodities. Unlocking the sector's strong multiplier effect on the economy would further contribute to increased incomes and poverty reduction.

Another important domain where Africa can profit is its biodiversity wealth, a unique opportunity for tourism. According to the United Nations' World Tourism Organization, Africa is one of the fastest-growing tourist destinations. There is already a growing recognition of the urgent need for the tourism industry, national governments, and international organisations to develop and implement strategies to face the changing climate conditions. Scaling up investments in ecotourism could mitigate tourism's environmental impact in the way the Gambia, Kenya, Rwanda, Zambia, Seychelles, and South Africa examples are demonstrating. Mastering the vast potential of its oceans and coasts can boost African economies significantly.

Preparing for and investing in climate change is costly. But not preparing for the same will prove to be catastrophic and even more expensive in the long run. Of all the regions of the world, Africa is believed to be the one causing the least harm to the global climate. Africa is a green continent, not necessarily in terms of colour, but in attitude. Its CO_2 emissions per capita are less than one ton per annum. It accounts for just 2.4% of the world's emissions. However, climate damage as a percentage of GDP is higher in Africa than observed elsewhere in the world. Despite the United Nations Framework Convention on Climate Change (UNFCCC), Africa remains a creditor of a massive ecological debt.

The UNFCCC must be congratulated for its relevance over the years and for elevating climate change issues to the highest political attention.

Thanks to it, developed countries have committed funds of US $100 billion a year by 2020 for climate finance, with the aim of developing countries under the Green Climate Fund. This is good, but it is not near enough.

Global emissions have risen, and major emitters are still not legally bound to reduce their emissions at the scale required to avoid irreversible climate change. Instead, those directly causing 80% of the global emissions are reversing the tide by rejecting the notion of an ecological debt. The amounts Africa receives for adaptation is negligible, in average less than 2% of the total. Economic development has not been at the forefront of climate negotiations and a 'loss and damage' account has never been agreed with. Is this compatible with the Africa we want?

The Conference of Parties (COP) that took place in Paris in November 2015 reached a comprehensive agreement on climate change. It has been celebrated as a major multilateral achievement. The truth though is that most of the agreement is non-binding. Although Paris presented an opportunity for Africa's voices to influence the debate, like demanding that research on 'loss and damage' from climate change-related disasters be funded, the results are not spectacular.

Going forward, climate justice discussions should be viewed by Africans from a pragmatic perspective. Many would argue that principles of corrective and distributive justice should apply. The expectations are that developed countries should take the lead and bear the burden in combating climate change, because they have been the major contributors to it in the past. Climate justice should not be reduced to a medium through which problems such as wealth distribution or correcting colonial injustices will all be addressed. It is only a matter of time before developing nations catch up with the developed world in cumulative emissions.

Climate justice is about advocating for a multidimensional type of justice that encompasses accountability. It is not solely concerned with equity in the distribution of environmental risks and benefits. There is a marked difference in the way climate disruption harms peoples' lives and livelihoods across cultures, communities, disciplines, nations, and regions of the globe. It involves acceptance of common but differentiated responsibilities, and the respective capabilities in relation to reduction of greenhouse gas emissions. The industrialised countries that are most responsible for greenhouse gas emissions and have most capacity to act must cut emissions first. After all, any well-designed climate change agreement must balance costs and benefits.

Climate change has been responsible for bad and good in the past. Most of it happened without humans having a clue why it was so. Now we know. To avoid the bad and aim for the good, Africa can take the lead. Africa should just not be a spectator. Its biggest opportunity is that it need not retrofit, but, rather, leapfrog. Taking all of these considerations into account, it only makes sense for Africa to focus on the Blue word and implement development plans in a way that enhances the greenness of its economy.

REFERENCES

AfDB, OECD, & UNDP. (2013). Structural Transformation and Natural Resources. *African Economic Outlook*. Paris: OECD Publishing.

AfDB, OECD, & UNDP. (2015). Regional Development and Spatial Inclusion. *African Economic Outlook*. Paris: OECD Publishing.

Brahmbhatt, M., Haddaoui, C., & Page, J. (2017). *Green Industrialisation and Entrepreneurship in Africa*. NCE Working Paper, Washington, DC.

Costanza, R., Hart, M., Posner, S., & Talberth, J. (Eds.). (2009). *Beyond GDP: The Need for New Measures of Progress*. Boston: University Creative Services.

ECA. (2016a). *Millennium Development Goals Report 2015: Assessing Progress in Africa Towards the Millennium Development Goals Lessons from the Millennium Development Goals Experience*. Addis Ababa: ECA.

ECA. (2016b). *Economic Report on Africa: Greening Africa's Industrialization*. Addis Ababa: ECA.

ECA. (2016c). *Africa's Blue Economy: A Policy Handbook*. Addis Ababa: ECA.

FAO. (2014). The Value of African Fisheries. *FAO Fisheries and Aquaculture*. Circular No. 1093, Rome: FAO.

Goldin, I. (Ed.). (2016). *Is the Planet Full?* Oxford: Oxford University Press.

Kelly, K. (2016). *The Investable: Understanding the 12 Technological Forces That Will Shape Our Future*. New York: Viking.

Kuznets, S. (1955). Economic Growth and Income Inequality. *American Economic Review, 49*(1–28), 1955.

CHAPTER 9

Inserting Agency in the Relations with China

Any analyst of the developments taking shape in the continent in the last decade and a half is bound to mention China. China's Africa policy is best analysed from its unique political and economic perspectives. Although China reaps considerable economic gains from Africa, it would be too simplistic to regard those benefits as the sole driver of China's international relations policy, concerning Africa. Analysts credit China's success in securing mineral rights in Africa to a wide range of economic instruments, particularly prestigious construction projects, financial assistance, and arms sales. The comprehensiveness of China's economic engagement and its willingness to defy risk perceptions make it a well-regarded partner (French 2014).

Tangible examples of modernisation, such as Chinese-built stadiums, highways, or foreign ministry buildings, have resonated well with African leaders who need to mobilise their populations, and who are often dissatisfied and frustrated with the slow pace of reform and economic development and have little patience for the rhetorical proclamations about prosperity in the future (French 2014; McKinsey Global Institute 2017).

In 1963, China sent its first medical team to Algeria. From the 1960s through to 2005, China sent more than 15,000 doctors to work in over four dozen countries, treating more than 180 million cases of HIV/ AIDS. Interestingly, one of the trends that has emerged prominently in response to the 2013 Ebola outbreak in West Africa was China's horizontal

© The Author(s) 2019
C. Lopes, *Africa in Transformation*,
https://doi.org/10.1007/978-3-030-01291-5_9

approach to healthcare, with an integrated system method, focusing on access to medicines and infrastructure.

In its inaugural development white paper, China reported sending a total of 256.29 billion yuan (US $38.54 billion) as aid to developing countries by the end of 2009. This included 106.2 billion yuan in grants, 76.54 billion yuan in interest-free loans, and 73.55 billion yuan in concessional loans. Additionally, China cancelled 25.58 billion yuan of debt stock. It is stated that 45.7% of China's aid went to Africa: that includes 1422 (non-investment) projects to some 50 recipient countries, between 2000 and 2011. According to their research, 62% of them provided information on committed financing amounting to an estimated US $75.4 billion of engagements.

In July 2012, at the fifth summit of the Forum on China-Africa Cooperation (FOCAC), China further committed US $5 billion in development funds as well as US $20 billion in form of credit lines. China also wrote off debt stocks for more than US $30 billion. In the FOCAC 2015 Summit, a further US $60 billion of investments for the next three years was announced by President Xi Jinping. If one compares these figures with the total OECD development aid to Africa of less than US $50 billion a year and a diminishing percentage of FDI stock, one gets an idea of the extension of China's largesse. However, if the comparison is with the amounts engaged by China in a myriad of other countries it is not so impressive. Pakistan alone is supposed to mobilise from China as much as Africa under the One Belt One Road initiative of the Chinese government.

Media outlets and Western scholars often suggest that China's relationship with Africa is built on its dependency on natural and energy resources as well as markets and investment opportunities for its booming industries and job-seeking workers. Indeed, China has often been criticised for taking advantage of Africa's vulnerability. This perception, nevertheless, fails to consider three important points.

First, China's more active engagement with Africa is part of its continuing emergence as a truly global player. It is no different from the traditional behaviour of any major power. In this context, China pursues its interests without hesitation and lends support without any 'strings attached'. Such relations are considered refreshing by many African political leaders.

Second, in its global and regional diplomacy, China, like all other great powers, is pursuing multiple objectives, including those that might create tensions between values and interests at both the national and global levels. China can no longer be expected to subordinate its commercial and strategic interests to others. Most African countries that have benefitted from China's increasing trade, investment, aid, and debt relief are not endowed with mineral wealth, offering fewer investment opportunities to Chinese enterprises. They are interesting to China for other reasons.

Third, the engagements of China with Africa are more market-driven than previously thought, not monopolised by government strategies. A multitude of actors, besides government, see Africa as an opportunity for their own business expansion and venture with their own innovative and risk-taking projects. There are 10,000 Chinese-owned firms operating in Africa right now, calling into question a monolithic view of the relationship. About 74% of the firms are optimistic about Africa (McKinsey Global Institute 2017).

According to a seminal McKinsey report (2017) the Chinese Government divides African countries in four categories: robust partners, solid partners, unbalanced partners, and nascent partners. The shades of grey are influenced by how much agency each partner exerts in relation to China. Ultimately, it is the responsibility of African leaders to devise a mutually beneficial relationship. What is important to retain is that a more nuanced view of the relationship reveals a two-way traffic indeed. The interest and urge of Africans to expand their presence in China is real, although less reported.

THE UNTOLD STORY OF AFRICANS IN CHINA

Since the 1970s, large numbers of Africans have migrated to foreign countries due to several reasons. Destinations for these migrants were typically the United States, Canada, and Western Europe, but small enclaves of Africans began to emerge in China after 2000. While contemporary China has always played host to relatively small numbers of African students and diplomatic personnel, the arrival of African migrants seeking permanent settlement was a new urban phenomenon for their host country (Li et al. 2009: 703). Data on African immigration to China is incomplete and vague at best, with estimates being few and far between (Bodomo 2012: 10) suggesting that there are some 5,00,000 Africans living in China, with 1,00,000 residing in Guangzhou alone, and the rest being spread out between Hong Kong, Macau, Yaw, Shanghai, Beijing, and some southern coastal, middle, and northern cities.

Particular to the large ethnic diaspora host city of Guangzhou, Africans are driven there due to its geographical location within the Chinese province of Guangdong—a large manufacturing base for goods that Africans cherish (Bodomo 2010: 698). Merchants have capitalised on the substantial availability of cheap goods, electronics, and other high-end products, which generate sizeable profits for African traders (Watts 2013).

Research works that focus on Nigerians in Guangzhou suggest that the attraction for going to China included relative ease of entry and its position as a possible springboard state for travel towards more desirable destinations (Haugen 2012: 71). With contacts and available finances, Nigerians and other immigrants have been able to use a migration 'broker' to smoothen their arrival into China. The brokers work with hotels and travel agents to obtain necessary supporting documents for visa applications and to regularise the stay of their clients.

Between 1996 and 2008, trade between Guangzhou and Africa rose from less than US $500 million annually to more than US $3 billion, with exports from the former increasing nearly ten-fold (Li et al. 2009: 704). Traditional enclaves for African migrants have been situated in the downtown area of Yuexiu district, near the city's administrative centre, now colloquially referred to by locals as the 'Chocolate Town' (Zhang 2008: 387). Among other factors, the rapidly expanding economic relationship between Africans and Guangzhou has created an abundance of opportunities for African migrant entrepreneurs, creating communities in the city (Li et al. 2009: 704).

Zhang (2008: 390) attributes the emergence of an African enclave in Guangzhou to an evolution of spatial dynamics at the neighbourhood level that represents a localised reaction to the changing market opportunities brought about by globalisation. In recent years, the Yuexiu district has been reshaped by the African diaspora traders, many of whom are perceived as a resource for revitalising neighbourhood commerce, fundamentally changing the economic and social dynamics of the city. If African traders were to vanish, there would likely be a significant ripple effect in pockets of South China's economy. Africans in Guangzhou may be the physical manifestation of what Bodomo (2010: 695) terms the 'immigrant community as bridge theory', whereby through their activities, African residents in this city might be, intentionally or not, serving as linguistic, cultural, and business connectors between their Chinese hosts and their home countries. This is further evidenced by the rising number of flights and the seating capacity of major African airline carriers, such as Egypt Air, Kenya Airways, Air Mauritius, Royal Air Maroc, Angola Airlines, South

African Airways, and, particularly, Ethiopian Airlines, which is flying daily to five Chinese cities and is soon to add a sixth one.

From the perspective of Africans in China, the growing relations are multifaceted. In 2006, Emmanuel Uwechue, a Nigerian-born engineer, achieved significant fame after performing in Mandarin on a popular Chinese reality television show, 'New Sights and Sounds'. Touring the country under the stage name 'Hao Ge', he has released numerous albums and has performed with a number of Chinese musical superstars (Wang 2011). While Uwechue is not the first foreigner to make a name in China, he is the first African to do so, with music industry experts crediting part of his success to close economic and cultural ties between China and Africa. Zimbabwean Vimbayi Kajese, who moved to Beijing in 2006, became the first African news presenter on the Chinese mainland English station of China Central Television (CCTV), the state-run media organisation. In 2012, CCTV, now CGTN, launched an African-affiliate station in Kenya, with the mandated objective of promoting 'communication and cooperation between China and African countries on politics, economy, trade, and culture' (Pengfei 2012). CGTN Africa has also been designated as a platform through which Chinese audiences can better understand Africa. *China Daily* followed the same pattern, and now it has an African edition published in Nairobi, with is content directed towards an African audience.

Education is another interesting area of expansion. According to Allison (2013) China, with its large national scholarship programme, was supporting an estimated 12,000 African students by covering fees, flights, accommodation, food, and monthly stipends. This number was in addition to roughly 18,000 self-supported African students in China (Allison 2013). More recent estimates point to over 50,000 students enrolled in Chinese universities though different modalities. Scholarship programmes play a key role in developing a positive brand among Africans. In the future, they may work for Chinese companies in their continent and spread 'good messages'. Similarly, China has pursued a branding or soft power advantage through the spread of its Confucius Institutes in Africa, with 25 already established at various universities across the continent (Kragelund 2014).

Chinese officials, in building their contemporary relationship with Africa, have argued that they want to engage every African country as an equal. Given this promise, Marsh (2014) argues that the vast majority of Africans in China view their presence in that country as a logical progression—a 'we are here because you are there' perspective to their relations.

As Fu Hualing, Head of the University of Hong Kong's Department of Law, notes, the Chinese are traditionally more used to dealing with rich Westerners. The influx of less-affluent Africans is entirely new (Law 2010). Despite the increasing volume of trade and the intimate political relations between China and numerous African governments, substantial ignorance, mistrust, and misunderstanding remain on a person-to-person basis (Baitie 2013).

Unlike Chinese contractors in Africa, migrants to China often arrive without any corporate or social backing (Law 2010). Some Chinese cite language barriers as impediments to broaching relationships and being prone to troublemaking. Others mention that many Chinese manifest xenophobic behaviours. The notable challenges encountered by many Africans in China certainly only reflect part of the local narrative.

A 2014 survey of some 204 traders from 50 African countries, carried out by the Guangzhou's *Southern Metropolis Daily*, found that about 18% of the respondents reported an average monthly income of 30,000+ Chinese yuan (US $4500+) from their business activities in the city. This figure is substantially higher than the 6647 Chinese yuan (US $1050+) average monthly income for white-collar workers in Guangzhou, as determined in the 2013–2014 regional wage research conducted on the Guangdong province by the Southern Talent Market. Most of the traders act on their own, increasing the perception of success. This is certainly a surprising development for Chinese local competitors. Slowly, it is influencing market behaviour towards African entrepreneurs and showing the potential the continent represents for Guangzhou's small and medium-scale enterprises.

CHINA'S ENGAGEMENT WITH AFRICA

Chinese Premier Li Keqiang (2014) published a newspaper editorial on what he saw as the characterisation of the relationship between China and Africa. He argued that Africa should be considered a 'pole' in a multipolar world, by virtue of its numerous seats at the United Nations, its vast land mass and natural resources endowment, and its status as the cradle of human civilisation, the place from which we have all come. Premier Keqiang characterises China and Africa as spiders, which can work together to 'tie down a lion', a metaphor implying the role both play in changing the international landscape. According to Premier Keqiang, four principles should define the deepening of this relationship:

- *First,* he argues for equality. In this context, he recalls the shared history, that of European colonisation. He points that China's aid to Africa will never have political strings.
- *Second,* he underlines the need for enhanced solidarity, mutual trust, and a deep respect for one another. China and Africa must support each another when faced with the turbulence of modern global politics.
- *Third,* he defends the joint pursuit of inclusive development, with China 'ready and willing' to share its knowledge, experience, expertise, and technology with Africa's developing states and its continental integrative organisations, including the AU.
- *Fourth,* he argues that China's engagement should not be limited to cooperation on the energy, resources, and infrastructure front, but, rather, it should expand into other sectors and areas. He suggests six areas for future cooperation: a regional cooperation plan; financial cooperation; collaborative poverty reduction; ecological and environmental protection; cultural exchanges; and enhanced security.

It would be good to inspect on what basis Chinese Premier Li Keqiang lands his ambitious goals.

China is the single largest trading partner of Africa, accounting for about 15% of the continent's trade, while Africa accounts for only 5% of Chinese trade. In 2010, China-Africa trade volume increased to US $114.18 billion, making China the continent's largest trading partner. In 2014, trade between Africa and China was worth US $221.5 billion, with imports (from China) and exports amounting to US $105.8 billion and US $115.7 billion respectively. This constitutes an increase of about 75% in Sino-African trade volume from 2010. African exports to China are mostly natural resources, while China exports mostly electrical and mechanical goods as well as consumer goods to Africa.

Even though Africa remains a relatively marginal player when it comes to China's overall trade with the rest of the world, its trading relationship with China has important implications for both parties.

Additionally, Chinese FDI to the continent increased from US $1.5 million in 1991 to US $20 billion by 2012. These impressive developments are not that old. The turning point came in 1993, when China went from being a net exporter to be a net importer of hydrocarbon products. By late 2004, the country had become the world's second-largest oil consumer, at

5.46 million barrels a day (bbl./d), outstripping Japan's 5.43 million bbl./d, and placing it behind the US 19.7 million bbl./d. By 2012, Chinese oil consumption had reached 10.22 million bbl./d, or 11.7% of the worldwide consumption. Moreover, the country was importing approximately 56% of the oil it consumed.

It is predicted that China's dependence on crude oil imports will continue to rise, reaching 65% by 2020. Indeed, over the past decade, China has doubled its oil consumption and is largely responsible for the growth of the consumption by non-OECD countries, from 37% in 1997 to almost 43% in 2007 (Monfort 2008). China surpassed the United States as the world's largest energy consumer in 2009, with oil accounting for slightly less than one-fifth of that amount. Its energy demands are expected to rise by 150% by 2020, even with a growth slowdown. However, new sources of energy can be tapped in China itself.

Energy experts point out that China's oil imports from Asia's oil producers have not been sufficient to meet its demands so far. Chinese officials are certainly aware of the limitation of Middle East oil and gas production but continue to heavily rely on it. In 2006, Angola surpassed Saudi Arabia as China's leading oil supplier, but the latest figure from 2014 shows that Saudi Arabia is back as the number one supplier. The Middle East collectively supplies 52% of Chinese crude oil, more than double of the African share (22%). While the energy market is crowded in that region, Africa Chinese investments in the sector face limited competition and are expanding significantly. The types of deals China can secure in Africa are also more attractive.

In fact, for more than a decade, China has sought access to Africa's rich energy and raw materials to fuel its surging economy. The Chinese leadership has always understood that the country's unprecedented growth required a continuous supply of raw materials, especially hydrocarbon fuels. The country's booming domestic energy demand, coupled with insufficient coal output and falling domestic crude oil production, prompted China to look overseas for stable supply sources.

The new wave of investments and interventions points in the direction of a rapid expansion away from raw materials and commodities. China, apart from being the number one trading partner, has also become the number one infrastructure financier and builder (with an amazing 50% of the international contracting from Africa), number one in FDI growth (already in one of the top spots if not attaining the first position on FDI stock), and third largest donor. Thirty per cent of Chinese firms are in manufacturing and they already represent about 12% of the continent-wide output in the sector.

CHINA AND AFRICA'S INDUSTRIALISATION

Africa serves as a low-value consumer market for Chinese goods, particularly for the loss-making state-owned enterprises, which have set up shop across the continent. The affordability of Chinese products fills an important gap in the market for many African consumers, who cannot afford more expensive, higher-quality consumer goods from Europe, and, given the inability of their own economies, cannot produce local equivalents. Prices of certain products have gone down up to 40% due to the Chinese firms' presence (McKinsey Global Institute 2017). Additionally, machinery and transport equipment imports are often linked to the strong presence of Chinese firms in the infrastructure sector, specifically telecommunications, road, and public construction (Renard 2014: 33). Furthermore, China and Africa both have stakes in whether African countries become viable production bases for labour-intensive manufacturing.

The share of manufactured goods in African exports to China (3%) is very low even compared to the exports to other destinations. Intra-Africa exports have a 40% share of manufactured goods, while the figures are 16% and 12% for exports to the 28-member states of the EU and the United States respectively. These numbers suggest that there is potential for African countries to move up the value chain in their trade, and in this regard, Chinese investment and expertise can help.

Africa is undergoing a manufacturing resurgence, with domestic manufacturing in Africa nearly doubling over the last ten years (AfDB et al. 2011). While agriculture, commodity exports, and services are still dominant outputs into the continental GDP, new industries in many parts of Africa are rapidly emerging. Examples include retail-clothing firms, such as H&M and Primark, which have started sourcing from Ethiopia; General Electric building, a US $250 million plant in Nigeria that manufactures electrical gear; Madecasse Chocolatier looking to add to its 650-people workforce in Madagascar that turns raw cocoa into premium chocolate products; Mobius Motors, a Kenyan firm, building cheap, durable automobiles for rough roads; Seemahale Telecoms of South Africa, producing cheap mobile phones. Other examples include Angola, building a weapons-manufacturing plant, and Morocco, creating more than 7000 new jobs in the aviation supply chain. These are all chief reckoners of the manufacturing boom (Oqubay 2015; McKinsey Global Institute 2017; Dollar 2016).

The rise of labour costs in China has created new opportunities for de-localisation of Pearl River low-value manufacturing to other regions of the world. The Chinese entrepreneurs have established the supply knowledge, have the necessary contacts with major world retailers, possess the capital and investment appetite to deal with difficult contexts, and can now replicate in the hubs in Africa what they master (Lin 2012; Monga and Lin 2015).

Historically, FDI from the developed world has been driven by privately owned enterprises, focused on obtaining maximum profit over a brief period of time and with the least amount of risk. Chinese FDI, however, is directed partially or wholly by state-owned enterprises, which are strategically placed with the objective of forming long-lasting rapports, assisted in part by their accessibility to national sources of capital. A large number of Chinese investments are linked, either implicitly or explicitly, to national strategic objectives, principally securing reserves of mineral resources for the Chinese industries back home. There is certainly a significant element of private profit-driven FDI from China, and profitability is far from being irrelevant, even for state-owned enterprises (Thrall 2015). Although up to 87% of Chinese firms pay tips to obtain licences and operate, they do not seem to be discouraged and are mostly profitable (McKinsey Global Institute 2017).

Chinese investors are good politicians who can adjust to the local context extremely quickly and are not perceived as expatriates with living standards way above the rest. They tend to be hard workers and instil into the market an entrepreneurial 'can do' attitude against adversity. The significant difference, however, is their perception of risk being very different from the one by traditional Western investors. These characteristics make China a good partner for the industrialisation policies being pursued by African countries and, thus, an important part of their plans for future development.

CHINA'S SUPPORT FOR AFRICAN REGIONAL INTEGRATION

Despite this bilateral focus, through its extensive cooperative trade and investment relations with Africa, China has played and is poised to continue playing a significant supportive role for Africa's regional integration. Most authors point to Chinese investment in infrastructure as the primary vehicle through which it can play this role. Indeed, some of the main challenges for further African integration and economic growth include inadequate transport, telecommunications, and power generation (Schiere 2011: 5). The African Infrastructure Country Diagnostic has estimated infrastructure financing requirements of US $93 billion per year over the next decade. China could be a key actor in a second generation of African regional integration, geared towards industrialisation. There are indications that this shift may already be occurring.

China has signed an agreement with the Economic Community of West African States (ECOWAS) for cooperation in infrastructure development, trade, and investment. While the agreement aimed at encouraging business cooperation, information exchange, bilateral training, and investment in natural resources, a key feature was the stimulation of infrastructure development, particularly the support for a trans-West African coastal highway, from Dakar to Lagos. Chinese infrastructure investment in ECOWAS has notably been driven by a parallel expansion of resource extraction agreements that require power and transportation of regional links (Bilal 2013: 43). At the continental level, China symbolically funded the construction of the AU headquarters in Addis Ababa. In January 2015, China signed a memorandum of understanding with the AU to support the development and construction of a new generation of road, rail, and air transport links between capital cities across the continent.

According to China's Information Office of the State Council's White Paper on China-Africa Economic and Trade Cooperation, China is firmly in support of achieving Africa's growth and development through the promotion of integration and continental unity (IOSC 2013: 14). The White Paper notes that since 2011, the Chinese government has signed framework agreements with the East African Community (EAC) and ECOWAS to explicitly expand and support cross-border infrastructure construction. China is a non-regional member of regional and continental organisations, including the African Development Bank, the West African Development Bank, and the Eastern and Southern African Trade and Development Bank. It has actively supported the African Development Fund's Multilateral Debt Relief Initiative for poverty reduction and regional integration on the continent (IOSC 2013: 14).

It is, thus, no secret that China supports African regional and continental integration, but whether this is only to serve its own economic objectives remains unclear. China's support comes not from a sense of altruism, but, as noted above, from a desire to remedy the political, technical, and geographical impediments to obtaining maximum dividends from investments. It will, therefore, be up to Africa to appropriately direct Chinese engagements in the right direction, and in support of their approved blueprints. Africa has a vision of how it would like to transform and build its future: achievement its continental Agenda 2063, the establishment of a Continental Free Trade Area (CFTA) by 2017 (indicative date), and the attainment of its stated African Development Goals. It is now important to walk the talk and make sure the continent's dialogue with China, through FOCAC or other vehicles, takes Africa's blueprints into full account.

FUTURE PARTNERSHIP DYNAMICS AND PROSPECTIVE DIFFICULTIES

China is well perceived by many African leaders, and even, in the most public views, despite generating a million permanent and temporary Chinese immigrants in the continent. The relationship becomes more complicated when one looks at perceptions beyond what African leaders may want to portray. Governments tend to have positive perceptions of the Chinese FDI, while recognising that Chinese enterprises may compete with local industries and business (Spring and Jiao 2008: 61).

In 2012, there was a marked rise in dissatisfaction with the Chinese in Ghana, despite a continued favourability of the relationship in opinion polls, manifested by increased anti-China sentiment amongst local populations as well as rash deportations of Chinese migrants (Aidoo 2014; Pew 2014). A survey of 1000 Cameroonians on the influx of Chinese investors and personnel into the country revealed a deep-seated distrust harboured for China (Spring and Jiao 2008: 62). However, that same survey also indicated that 92% of those interviewed held positive views of China as being 'good' for Cameroon's economy (Rebol 2010: 3526). Rebol concludes that different African perceptions of China are primarily the result of the diverse roles that China has played in the continent, depending on local circumstances and strategic objectives (Rebol 2010: 3526).

When viewed as a provider of consumer goods, critique arises as Chinese entrepreneurs begin to push out local businesses, particularly retailers who previously imported from China to resell at home. Chinese investments have been accused by some as having low environmental, labour, and safety standards, and/or harsh working conditions, while large-scale infrastructure projects are said to rarely employ locals. There is criticism that

Chinese investment in natural resources has made it increasingly difficult for African states to diversify their economies (Rebol 2010: 3526–3527).

The Western media bias against China's growing influence on the continent equates the latter's moves to a new scramble for the continent's riches (Dollar 2016). The weight of such views in Africa itself is palpable, given the dominance of external public opinion in the continent. Despite many attempts to correct such a skewed narrative, the reality remains that these views are more widespread than the leaders in the continent would admit.

Over the last decade, China-African relations have been primarily dictated by China's interest in Africa's natural resources, and its ability to support that interest with a cash-for-resources policy. Going forward, however, it will become critical for African leaders to become more strategic in their relationship by articulating a unified China policy. There is a sense of urgency to operate this shift. In the past, China has sought to use Africa as a raw material source to fuel its own growth, but now that it has emerged as an economic superpower, its interests will likely begin to change, thereby limiting the effect of any resource-based leverage that the African countries may still hold (Songwe and Moyo 2012: 3).

As China shifts gradually from an investment-led to a consumer-driven model of growth, its economic interests abroad will change. This offers a unique opportunity for African countries that possess or formulate forward-looking policies for diversifying their economies. Many can leverage their comparative natural resource endowment for commodity-based industrialisation. Given the growing closeness of these two economies, the current structural change in China exposes African economies to risks as well as opportunities.

China's slowdown in 2014–2015 has hit commodity markets hard. China, which accounts for nearly half of global metal consumption, has witnessed a decline in industrial activity and a consequential moderation in demand, consistent with its structural transformation. In fact, for the first time in over a decade, OECD countries have rebounded as a net source of growth for metals (The World Bank 2015). For most commodity-dependent countries, though, price volatility has been more problematic than their long-run decline. Unprocessed commodities have a higher volatility than processed minerals, particularly for ores and metals, with annual fluctuation in prices ranging around 23% for unprocessed, while only 13% for processed ores.

The rebalancing in China presents transformative opportunities for Africa to climb higher up the value chain through greater beneficiation and processing of its ores. As a result of commitments towards diversification of their economies, African countries have been able to weather the falling prices of commodities, better than what was weathered in the past.

While recent global economic forecast downgrades many resource-rich African countries, their sectoral composition and source of GDP are changing faster than what is acknowledged by many pundits. Over two recent boom periods in commodity prices, industry and manufacturing output together expanded faster than the rest of the continental economy (ECA 2015). For example, the 5.1% growth rate experienced in 2013 by Angola, Africa's second-largest oil producer and second-largest oil exporter to China, came mostly from construction and industry. In fact, other sectors are taking the slack, suggesting an even greater potential for African economies to turn their resource advantage into competitive engine for driving industrialisation.

Endowed with world-class deposits of economy-transforming minerals, Africa stands with comparative advantage to attract investment as well as a deep knowledge of processing and beneficiation imported from China. In the past decade, China has slashed the number of its aluminium producers to 64 from its original 120, and is unlikely to remove its 15% export taxes.

There is one significant red flag about the difficulties a commodity-based industrialisation strategy will face from China. If Africa tries to climb the global value chains it will have to bear in mind China's own interests in that regard. China can slow down some major projects it is involved with and not commit to others that can enhance undesirable competition for them.

Due to lack of investment, power infrastructure remains the limiting factor for industrialisation. Several existing projects to expand energy access and many others under consideration will depend on Chinese interest. The unreliable supply of electricity makes Africa lose 3–5% of GDP every year (ECA 2014). Any transformation agenda will be hampered by the chronic shortage of electricity. In fact, if Africa were to refine all base metals alone, it will require almost 115% of the total electricity it currently produces (ECA 2013). Chinese investments in the power sector are more than welcomed.

China can be a player in the production of clean energy in Africa. That will certainly support Africa's leapfrogging but also the leadership of Chinese firms in this frontier market and value chain. Africa has enormous renewable energy potential to produce clean energy to meet its growing needs along with allowing for development and industrialisation (Lopes 2014). The continent's hydropower capacity of 1852 Twh per year can satisfy its needs through power pooling and cross-border power trade. Africa has an average uniform 325 days of bright sunlight per year, receiving 2000 kilowatt-hours per square metre per year. The wind and wave power potential along the west coast exceeds 3750 kilowatt-hours. Significant geothermal potential in the Eastern Rift Valley stretches to about 3700 miles in length, with the potential in Kenya alone estimated at 10,000 megawatts.

Energy is just one example, though. Simply put China needs Africa as much as Africa needs China. The relationship looks like a Faustian bargain, whereby Africa is jeopardising its long-term economic health for quick short-term fixes. Africa, in its partnership with China, can help support at least six of its core interests: infrastructure development; FDI; achieving favourable loan terms; the reduction of debt; the sustaining of high growth rates; an expansion of its trade volume to accelerate its economic development; and sourcing innovative technology and professionalised training (Haroz 2011: 73–75).

Clearly, Africa would like to be more than a source for raw material exports. It offers a market that could benefit from China's technological innovation and increasing outsourcing of low-tech manufacturing activities.

African elites have no incentives to change their dealings with China if they enjoy considerable control of a state's government apparatus that allows their illegitimate access to resources and the public sentiment in favour of Chinese investment lacks scrutiny. Thus, what Africa 'hopes to get' out of a relationship with China requires a shift of the current mindset as some reform-minded governments are, fortunately, demonstrating.

While African states have greater leverage in dealing with China, thanks to their natural resources, this has not been converted into negotiating power, as the categorisation of countries by the Chinese demonstrates (McKinsey Global Institute 2017). It is paramount that each African country as well as the regional entities clearly defines their China policy. Given the focus placed by most African institutions and governments on industrialisation, as a means for attaining structural transformation, China looks like an obvious partner. As the saying goes, the devil is in the details.

144   C. LOPES

REFERENCES

AfDB, OECD, & UNDP. (2011). New Opportunities for African Manufacturing. *African Economic Outlook*. Paris: OECD Publishing.
Aidoo, R. (2014, October 25). China's "Image" Problem in Africa. *The Diplomat*. Retrieved May 15, 2015, from http://thediplomat.com/2012/10/non-interference-a-double-edged-sword-for-china-in-africa/?allpages=yes.
Allison, S. (2013, July 5). Fixing China's Image in Africa, One Student at a Time. *The Guardian*. Retrieved May 6, 2016, from http://www.theguardian.com/world/2013/jul/31/china-africa-students-scholarship-programme.
Baitie, Z. (2013, August 28). On Being African in China. *The Atlantic*. Retrieved May 17, 2015, from http://www.theatlantic.com/china/archive/2013/08/on-being-african-in-china/279136/.
Bilal, S. (2013). External Influences on Regional Integration in West Africa: The Role of Third Parties. In R. Sohn & A. K. Oppong (Eds.), *Regional Trade and Monetary Integration in West Africa and Europe* (pp. 33–56). Bonn: Center for European Integration Studies.
Bodomo, A. (2010). The African Trading Community in Guangzhou: An Emerging Bridge for Africa–China Relations. *The China Quarterly, 203*, 693–707.
Bodomo, A. (2012). *Africans in China – A Sociocultural Study and Its Implications on Africa-China Relations*. Amherst: Cambria Press.
Dollar, D. (2016). *China's Engagement with Africa: From Natural Resources to Human Resources*. Washington, DC: Brookings Institution.
ECA. (2013). *Millennium Development Goals Report 2013: Assessing Progress in Africa Towards the Millennium Development Goals Food Security in Africa – Issues, Challenges and Lessons*. Addis Ababa: ECA.
ECA. (2014). *Economic Report for Africa: Dynamic Industrial Policy in Africa*. Addis Ababa: ECA.
ECA. (2015). *Economic Report on Africa: Industrializing Through Trade*. Addis Ababa: ECA.
French, H. (2014). *China's Second Continent: How a Million Migrants Are Building a New Empire in Africa*. New York: Vintage Books.
Haroz, D. (2011). China in Africa: Symbiosis of Exploitation. *Fletcher Forum of World Affairs, 35*(2), 65–88.
Haugen, H. Ø. (2012). Nigerians in China: A Second State of Immobility. *International Migration, 50*(2), 65–80.
IOSC. (2013). *China-Africa Economic and Trade Cooperation (2013)*. Beijing: IOSC.
Keqiang, H. L. (2014). *Bring About a Better Future for China–Africa Cooperation*. Ministry of Foreign Affairs of the People's Republic of China. Retrieved May 15, 2015, from http://www.fmprc.gov.cn/mfa_eng/wjdt_665385/zyjh_665391/t1154397.shtml.

Kragelund, P. (2014). *Chinese Soft Power and Higher Education in Africa: The Confucius Institute at the University of Zambia.* Proceedings of the 14th EADI General Conference, 23–26 June 2014, Bonn, pp. 1–21.

Law, V. (2010, November 25). China Welcomes Growing African Trade, but Not the Africans Who Facilitate It. *Christian Science Monitor.* Retrieved May 13, 2015, from http://www.csmonitor.com/World/Asia-Pacific/2010/1125/China-welcomes-growing-African-trade-but-not-the-Africans-who-facilitate-it.

Li, Z., Ma, L. J. C., & Xue, D. (2009). An African Enclave in China: The Making of a New Transnational Urban Space. *Eurasian Geography and Economics, 50*(6), 699–719.

Lin, J. (2012). *The Quest for Prosperity: How Developing Economies Can Take Off.* Princeton, NJ: Princeton University Press.

Lopes, C. (2014). *Powering Africa's Industrialisation and Agricultural Revolution with Renewable Energies.* Retrieved May 20, 2015, from http://www.unep.org/ourplanet/2014/June/PDF/EN/article11.pdf.

Marsh, J. (2014, July 1). African Migrants Let Down by the Chinese Dream. *Al-Jazeera.* Retrieved May 15, 2015, from http://america.aljazeera.com/opinions/2014/7/africans-inchinachinesemigrantsinafricachinaafricarelations.html.

McKinsey Global Institute. (2017). *Dance of Lions and Dragons.* London, New York: MGI.

Monfort, J. (2008). *Oil Consumption Continues Slow Growth.* Working Paper, World Watch Institute.

Monga, C., & Lin, J. (Eds.). (2015). *The Oxford Handbook of Africa and Economics* (Vol. 2). Oxford: Oxford University Press.

Oqubay, A. (2015). *Made in Africa.* Oxford: Oxford University Press.

Pengfei, Z. (2012, January 11). About CCTV Africa. *CNTV.com.* Retrieved May 15, 2015, from http://english.cntv.cn/program/africalive/20120111/117620.shtml.

Pew. (2014). *Global Indicators Database.* Ghana. Retrieved July 20, 2017, from http://www.pewglobal.org/database/indicator/71/country/82/.

Rebol, M. (2010). Public Perceptions and Reactions: Gauging African Views of China in Africa. *African Journal of Agricultural Research, 5*(25), 3524–3535.

Renard, T. (2014). Strategic Prudence: The European Union and the Shanghai Cooperation Organization. In *PRI/HSF, SCO's Role in Regional Stability: Prospects of Its Expansion* (pp. 38–51). Islamabad: IPRI.

Schiere, R. (2011). China and Africa: An Emerging Partnership for Development? In *China and Africa: An Emerging Partnership for Development* (pp. 1–12). Tunis: African Development Bank.

Songwe, V., & Moyo, N. (2012). China-Africa Relations: Defining New Terms of Engagement. In Z. Lewis & B. Routman (Eds.), *Foresight Africa – Top Priorities for the Continent in 2012.* Washington: Brookings Institution.

Spring, A., & Jiao, Y. (2008). *China in Africa: African Views of Chinese Entrepreneurship*. Global and Local Dynamics in African Business and Development 9th Annual International Conference, University of Florida Gainesville. Mimeo.

Thrall, L. (2015). *China's Expanding African Relations: Implications for US Security*. Santa Monica: Rand.

Wang, J. (2011, March 15). Nigerian Finds Pop Stardom in Beijing. *The New York Times*.

Watts, E. (2013, August 8). A 'Little Africa' in Southern China. *The Diplomat*. Retrieved May 21, 2015, from http://thediplomat.com/2013/08/a-little-africa-in-southern-china/.

The World Bank. (2015). *Commodity Markets Outlook*. Second Quarter Report, Washington, DC: World Bank.

Zhang, L. (2008). Ethnic Congregation in a Globalizing City: The Case of Guangzhou, China. *Cities, 25*(6), 383–395.

CHAPTER 10

Conclusions

Africa had to face a stream of sad news in 2017. President Buhari's extended stay in London for medical reasons made Nigerians wonder whether his health would allow him to run a country with an array of critical challenges, from Boko Haram terrorism to economic difficulties. In Egypt renewed and deadly attacks in the Sinai raised alarm and got Egyptians guessing whether they would have more instability and repression in the country. In South Africa debates around corruption, state capture, and poor service delivery by government agencies got the rand spinning and South Africans discussing about future direction of the country. In Algeria the evaporation of the largest African sovereign reserves was the most visible impact of the lack of economic reforms capable of propelling a more diversified economy. Sudan remained enmeshed in too many internal conflicts while fighting for international recognition. Angola, like Nigeria, was struggling with the pervasive effects of the chaos provoked by the sudden drop of oil export earnings, in the middle of a long-awaited leadership transition.

These six countries correspond to more than 60% of Africa's GDP. If they cough the continent gets fever. No wonder why they play such a major role shifting the narratives back to the old-fashioned scepticism. The 'Africa rising' story line changed fast, caught by facts that started to reverse the faith of those who predicted Africa as a region poised for sustainable growth.

For the many Africans that never liked the simplicity with which the continent is judged—and the latest narratives confirmed—being trashed is

© The Author(s) 2019
C. Lopes, *Africa in Transformation*,
https://doi.org/10.1007/978-3-030-01291-5_10

more common than being praised. After all, 'Africa rising' was about opportunities for the world market, not necessarily focusing on the interests of Africa itself. This book tried to offer the reader an alternative view about the continent's challenges. Hopefully it has provided a background for assessing complexity and identifying what can be done to transform Africa.

On the *political front* there is a need to heed the call of the citizens themselves. In the IIAG (2015) there is a remarkable finding: between 2006 and 2015 no less than 37 countries hosting 70% of the continent's population have registered governance improvements. Yet two-thirds of the countries, or 67% of the population, have registered a deterioration of the freedom of expression. Equally disappointing were the negative trends for safety and rule of law and corruption, while accountability scored the lowest in the indicators of performance.

Afrobarometer surveys, used by IIAG, are even more specific: 'Most Africans feel at least "somewhat free" to join any political group they want. But only 21 of 36 countries surveyed have majorities who feel "completely free", with some countries observing seen sharp declines in perceived freedom' (Afrobarometer 2016b). Freedom of association is central to other freedoms. Those who believe they can associate also most likely feel they can speak, write, or vote freely. However, there is a nuance worth noting. One in every three Africans says governments have the right to ban organisations that go against their policies (Afrobarometer 2016b).

More than half of the Africans leave in functional multiparty democracies. In a graphic demand and supply visualisation, Afrobarometer (2016a) concluded 43% of Africans were demanding more than they were getting while 35% were supplied more than they were demanding.

The tension between old forms of representation and attitudinal changes provoked by democratisation of information access is likely to catapult African politics into a very different compass in the next few years and way into the future. Neo-patrimonial type of leaders and systems, based on rent-seeking, has been responsible for the lack of structural transformation. One cannot discuss commodities and their vicious addictions without looking into the economic colonial patterns, the type of regimes that were established after independence, and the rounding up of African countries to conform to a certain view of development that did not allow them to integrate modern systems of production and get out of the commodity trap. This is now a task Africans are apparently ready to confront. Leaders that deliver services and development are being praised and in turn are deriving their legitimacy from being capable of delivering. Their authoritarian bend is never welcomed but often it is tolerated, if they deliver. On the other hand leaders that are ineffectual are being pressured and struggle to last.

The debate about the nature of democracy in Africa will be influenced by the elements above. Some key aspects deserve to be highlighted. International human rights instruments are a good reference to continue to keep governments on check and oblige them to account. But they are not enough. Youth participation and modern forms of interaction call for innovative participatory formats for consultation and decision-making. Tools for transparency and evaluation are readily available. Electoral integrity is technically attainable if there is predisposition to introduce adequate tools. Most African countries will have to respond to such expectations.

On the issue of *respecting diversity* improvements in the way civic engagement is organised and promoted will go a long way to reduce minority, vulnerable, and marginalised groups' acceptance of institutions, electoral systems, and power distribution arrangements. Currently the deficit of trust is wide (ECA 2009).

In the name of pan-Africanism nationalist ideology has been used to supress dissent. The imported model of nation-state is now collapsing. Federalism is gaining ground. Officially only Nigeria, Ethiopia, Sudan, South Sudan, Somalia, and Comoros are federal states (although with weaknesses that are the subject of vast literature). However, the movement towards decentralisation and recognition of cultural and other peculiarities is gaining ground and may result in changes for many unitary states.

Another option to respect diversity is to enshrine principles relating to the recognition of differences in the constitutional arrangements. Morocco and Algeria recently changed their Constitution to include the Amazigh language as an official language. South Africa recognises no less than 11 languages as official. Some of the tension in the electoral and political systems of demographically important countries such as Cameroon, Kenya, or the Democratic Republic of the Congo is linked to distrust that minorities are protected.

As ECA stated:

African countries are essentially plural societies—of diverse identities, groups, classes and professional interests—state formation and the emergent political architecture exacerbated the challenge of managing diversity in

Africa. Diversity is best managed in an enabling democratic framework, in which all people are at liberty to choose their leaders and programmes through free, fair, credible and regular elections. Yet at the time, authoritarian political structures were grafted onto previous policies of ethnic and social fragmentation that had aimed to divide groups and generate antagonism, necessary for colonial economic exploitation and political dominance. (ECA 2009: 4)

Countries that want to embark on structural transformation cannot ignore the political difficulties that will result from tensions generated by lack of representation in the sharing of power and economic benefits. This is not a superficial image-building exercise. It requires levels of commitment that have to be translated into specific policies with appropriate checks and balances.

In order to *increase policy space* governments will have to demonstrate that they are well managed. Good governance performance gets noticed. Despite the declining ODA role, the actors active in that field are powerful opinion makers. They look at these issues carefully associating with success and dissociating themselves from trouble. Africa may well depend more on FDI, remittances, or domestic consumption for its financial resources; still the story line in the mainstream media is captured by ODA specialists and international institutions devoted to aid.

Bretton Woods institutions and Washington-based think tanks continue to set the tone in regard to the interpretations of what African countries should do, or whether some of the alternative pathways should be considered sound or not.

The only possibility for African countries to expand their space is through the persistent demonstration that alternatives are possible and are sound. The best way to do so is by assessing the narratives constructed in Washington or other centres of power, verify their consistency or possible contradictions, and compare with treatment offered to other countries and regions in similar situations. Being right after some time elapses matters little as these organisations move on with the trends and can happily join the critics of what they recommended or did after the facts proved a different course of action or outcome was more suitable.

There is a wind of freedom in the economics field epitomised by the choice of Richard Thaler for the 2017 Nobel Prize for the discipline. Thaler is a prominent advocate of economics being about people, not blind theories. He defends simplicity, nudging rather than nagging (Thaler and Sunstein 2009). Africans have been taking advantage of wider policy variety but not enough. They need to nudge the powerful to change them too. On trade their agency is missing in action. On global macrodiscussions their voice is absent. This can change. Without gaining space it will be difficult to defend Africa's time.

The imperative of *structurally transform through industrialisation* will define the fortunes of the continent. With the odds against such transformation, at a time of reduced value for manufactured goods and importance of labour, Africa enters the twenty-first century with all the characteristics of a latecomer. Using the windows of opportunity will require a combination of three governance directions:

- Ambition, without which most countries will not be able to plan in accordance with major demographic shifts and increasing competition. Successful performance is now linked to the leadership of countries that have been able to predict developments and anticipate shocks. It is a new form of resilience; the resilience that allows to keep the ambitious path despite setbacks that are likely to occur, be it drought, extreme weather, exchange rates, or commodity prices variations.
- Consistency or coherence across national actors, particularly government. Industrialisation requires a comprehensive industrial policy, which in turn means it has to be a national priority, not the affair of the 'Ministry of Industry'. However, comprehensiveness is not about rigidity. There is a need for a dynamic and speedier interaction between government and private agents such as local champions or external investors and financiers. The flexibility goes hand in hand with focus and clear-set objectives and targets. If each agency's priority is aligned with national goals, things move faster, impress potential investors, and grow the attractiveness of the sector or country. For example, ministries in charge of human capital development cannot be dissociated from the centrality of economic policy and have to cease to be considered as spenders confined to social protection alone.
- Sophistication is the third element of the successful trinity. With the current levels of globalisation of most value chains it is impossible to position a country in ignorance of the impact of the said chains in their policy choices and moves. For instance, if a country wants to have a higher level of value-addition on a given soft commodity, let

us say cocoa or coffee, it needs to know the role of international traders. If the aim is to be a player in the garments industry, transports and logistics are a major part of the cost structure.

As some examples presented in the book demonstrate several countries have understood the difficult path towards industrialisation. In order to succeed it will be necessary to have more than just determination or invest in infrastructure. There is a need to embrace levels of complexity and upgrade decision-making processes that match the multifarious nature of our globalised world.

In the continent *boosting agricultural productivity* continues to be the most obvious entry point for such structural transformation. The alliance between agriculture and industrialisation is based on the need to modernise and formalise economic systems. The focus on green revolutions is welcome, but insufficient. Africa's focus on agriculture has been mostly social, not economic. Changing that pattern will require some major champions and a lot more specialisation in many domains.

The examples of countries in Asia and Latin America show that with the right combination of land tenure, adapted science experiments and innovation, and access to finance, improvements can be quick. With abundance of land there is no reason Africa needs to make a choice between commercial farming and smallholder producers. It can and should have both. Agri-business, a strong creator of modern jobs, prospers with an abundance of suppliers and predictable crops. Current overdependence on weather can be turned around with irrigation and renewable energy provision. The future of agriculture depends on demographic transitions that are managed, not traumatic. The establishment of new continuums between rural and urban spaces is likely to define Africa's modernity.

Africans will require a new *social contract* that recognises their demographic transition as completely different from previous historically significant youth bulges. The African one is taking place at a time the planet is going to witness a spectacular and *extra*-ordinary population ageing. Intergenerational solidarity will have to be reinterpreted when older people will live geographically very distant from younger people.

There is universal acclaim to the concept of sustainable development without measuring the full impact of demographics in it. The discussions about the future of work, technological changes, and regulation or new forms of attributing value tend to protect asset owners that are ageing against younger agents that are dispossessed, but knowledgeable. Africans have to seize this debate before everyone else. They can do it through the discussions on environment protection as well as on the polarised issue of human mobility.

Because *climate change* is likely to define more than any other mega-trend the future of the planet, the stakes for Africa should go way beyond the confined space of climate adaptation. Africans should take the lead on a number of fronts. While doing so they should use the argument of climate justice but not narrowly interpreted to signify the need to compensate the least polluters they have been. It should be about the need to be central in the definition of the future because they were the least polluters, true, but more because they have and will continue to have for the foreseeable future the youngest population. More than any other continent they are concerned about a preserved planet for the future.

Gains obtained in negotiations of international environmental agreements have so far been very timid. Areas not yet mastered by such negotiations such as the blue economy offer the best option for Africans to gain ground and make a dent. Leapfrogging in areas such as green industrialisation of sustainable infrastructure should be prioritised as well as the costs associated with such choices are likely to be less onerous than retrofitting old industries and infrastructure.

The key partner for Africa to realise many of its objectives is probably China.

Inserting agency in the relations with China will for the years to come influence more than any other relationship whether Africa will expand its role in the world economy. The diversified economic engagements and multifaceted roles Chinese-owned enterprises and the Government of China already play in the continent overwhelm the interventions and presence of any other partner. The speed of expansion is likely to be accelerated by the new global initiatives of the Chinese Government such as 'One Belt One Road'. Africa offers also an easy market brand positioning for China (French 2014).

The type of interaction between China and Africa is currently defined by the former in terms that favour those who are sophisticated and prepared (McKinsey Global Institute 2017) to deal with them. African agency in the relations with the strategic friend has been exerted convincingly by only a handful of African countries so far. The elements of what constitutes a good strategy are based on the realisation of the Chinese economic interests combined with local potential and ambition.

Some of the negotiations Africans embarked upon with other partners will limit the scope of what they can do with China. A good example is the EU-led trade-related Economic Partnership Agreements. It will be contradictory for Africans to increase policy space with IFIs just to be limited by the nature of the trade agreements they are signing. The Chinese are watching and are likely to judge Africans' proclamations about the desire for regional integration on face value.

If Africans take these challenges seriously, they will influence not only their future and the present but also the entire planet.

REFERENCES

Afrobarometer. (2016a). *PP36: Do Africans Still Want Democracy?* Published 22 November 2017. Retrieved October 13, 2017, from http://globalreleases. afrobarometer.org/global-release/pp36-do-africans-still-want-democracy.

Afrobarometer. (2016b). *AD128: After 50 Years, Freedom of Association Is Firmly Established, Though Far from Absolute, in Africa.* Published 16 December 2016. Retrieved October 13, 2017, from http://globalreleases.afrobarometer. org/global-release/ad128-after-50-years-freedom-association-firmly-established-though-far-absolute.

ECA. (2009). *African Governance Report II.* Oxford: Oxford University Press.

French, H. (2014). *China's Second Continent: How a Million Migrants Are Building a New Empire in Africa.* New York: Vintage Books.

IIAG. (2015). *Ibrahim Index of African Governance 2015.* London: Mo Ibrahim Foundation.

McKinsey Global Institute. (2017). *Dance of Lions and Dragons.* London, New York: MGI.

Thaler, R., & Sunstein, C. R. (2009). *Nudge: Improving Decisions About Health, Wealth, and Happiness.* New York: Penguin.

INDEX

© The Author(s) 2019
C. Lopes, *Africa in Transformation*,
https://doi.org/10.1007/978-3-030-01291-5